The Vinegar Book

by

Emily Thacker

First published in Great Britain in 1995 by Carnell Ltd.
28 Eccleston Square, London SW1V 1NZ

Typeset and design by Tangent Graphics, London N16 0DP

ISBN 1 85779 826 0

Contents

Introduction   7

Chapter One: **Stay Young Forever!**   9

Chapter Two: **Vinegar Fights Disease**   17

Chapter Three: **Where Did Vinegar Come From?**   45

Chapter Four: **Vinegar's Historic Development**   53

Chapter Five: **Vinegar Making**   67

Chapter Six: **In A Pickle And Proud Of It**   78

Chapter Seven: **Cooking With Vinegar**   90

Chapter Eight: **What's New?**   99

Appendix I: **What Does Cider Vinegar Contain?**   107

Appendix II: **Useful Addresses**   109

Thank You!   110

Introduction

D ear Reader, I can't begin to tell you how many kind people have written to tell me how cider vinegar has been a part of better health and easier cleaning.

In reading my post, it seems as if many readers feel cider vinegar is practically an instant remedy for all the ills of human kind! Some believe it is a liquid cure-all — a tonic to extend life, promote good health, and provide necessary vitamins, amino acids and trace elements. Faith in the power of cider vinegar dates back to about the time of the discovery of the apple. And, some of the claims made for it seem a bit extravagant.

Do l feel cider vinegar is a remedy for all the ills of this world? Well, probably not.

But vinegar does contain a multitude of essential trace elements, many of which science has not decided a value for. The importance of trace elements continues to be uncovered by medical researchers. And evidence continues to mount that pure, natural foods are our best source for both minerals and vitamins. The latest findings show the number of elements and compounds in a good cider vinegar make the ingredient list of most multi-vitamins look paltry by comparison.

So perhaps the future will reveal how vinegar helps promote good health. And for sure, it is a good, safe, recognised cleaner. It is kind to the planet and it protects the environment.

If you want to radiate good health and well being for as many decades as possible, you should look very carefully at your diet and lifestyle. How you conduct your life can ensure a more radiant, abundant future. Most illness in individuals over 50 is due to degenerative diseases: arthritis, cancer, and cardiovascular disturbances like heart attacks and strokes. And most doctors agree these are diseases which are affected by what you eat and how you live.

Through the ages, many have felt that cider vinegar could play a part in a healthy lifestyle. You cannot control your medical history or genes. They create within you certain tendencies and weaknesses. But you can control some of your future. You control what you eat and how much exercise you get. This is the only body you have, so you better take care of it. And that's what this book is about — some preventive maintenance.

Beyond that, much of what this book does is relate history. The interpretation must be left to you.

Do remember, traditional remedies have value, but they cannot take the place of medical advice. When you are ill, you should seek the advice of a doctor. For everyday healthy living and cleaning, you may want to try some of these traditional vinegar tips.

Emily

Chapter One

Stay Young Forever!

So you want to live forever! Cider vinegar contains the healthy goodness of apples, concentrated into a teaspoon of golden liquid. It is packed with essential amino acids and health-giving enzymes. So it comes as no surprise that some people have claimed this natural source of vitamins and minerals will cure all that ails mankind — and even extend life and youthfulness.

Is cider vinegar an instant remedy for all the ills of this world? A magical nostrum? A mystical elixir? A liquid cure all? Some believe it is something very close to this!

Conventional medical systems are sickness oriented — designed to respond to illness. But good health, and extending the prime of life, begins with a body that is maintained, every single day, by a good diet and healthy activities. A healthy, ageless body requires a diet rich in a wide assortment of nutrients. And the safest way to get adequate nutrients is to supply the body with a varied diet. It should meet all known nutritional requirements and contain a lot of trace elements.

Perhaps this is why cider vinegar has the reputation of being an almost magical tonic — one of the most health-giving, nutrient-filled fluids known to mankind. A teaspoon of this golden liquid supplies a generous portion of the building blocks needed to be a healthy person! This potent substance is endowed with a multitude of vitamins, minerals and essential amino acids.

Scientists know humans need very tiny amounts of hundreds of as yet largely unidentified compounds. Nutritional researchers are constantly discovering minerals, enzymes, amino acids, and other substances that the body needs for complete health. Exactly how the body uses these trace elements remains a medical mystery. Nor has science identified the amount needed of most of them.

- Doctors do know that a tiny deficiency, a missing milli-micro-gram of an important element, can result in sickness, premature ageing, or loss of mental acuity. The best advice nutritional scientists can give us is that we should eat a wide range of foods, making a broad spectrum of nutrients available to the body.

Since the dawn of time mankind has sought the magic elixir which bubbles from the *Fountain of Youth*. For most of us, cider vinegar may be as close as we'll ever come to such a universal remedy. The secret of eternal youth is already ours. It is simply to be vital and to be able to enjoy a vigorous active life every single day we live.

So it is no wonder that cider vinegar is a time-honoured prescription for those of us who want to retain vitality and good health well into old age. Throughout the ages it has been prescribed as an aid in maintaining general health, preventing disease, controlling weight, easing the discomfort of coughs, colds and breathing difficulties, and settling a disturbed digestive system.

- Because traditional remedies (like those in this book) are handed down from parent to child to grandchild over many generations, changes occur. Families develop their own variations. Yet, there is one constant theme: some small amount of cider vinegar, taken each day, somehow brings better health and longer life. Some of these traditional health measures follow:

LIVE A LONG, HEALTHY, VITAL LIFE

Ensure long life and health by drinking vinegar every day. Simply add a tablespoon to a full glass of water and drink it down.

The way to stay healthy and alert, well into old age, is to combine 1 teaspoon of vinegar, 1 teaspoon of honey, and full glass of water. Take this tonic 3 times a day, half an hour before meals.

For a long, vigorous life, filled with robust good health, sip a vinegar tonic, very slowly, before each meal. Mix together and begin drinking immediately: 1 cup of warm water, 2 tablespoons of cider vinegar, and 1 teaspoon of honey.

- The most palatable way to take a daily dose of vinegar is to add a small dollop of clover honey to a tablespoon of vinegar and a teaspoon of olive oil. Mix together and drip this healthy dressing over a small bowl of green salad.

A health-promoting salad dressing can be made from ¼ cup of vinegar, ¼ cup of corn oil, and ½ cup of honey. Mix well and serve with the evening meal to keep the whole family in good health.

Memory can be greatly improved by drinking a glass of warm water with a teaspoon of cider vinegar stirred in before each meal.

FIGHT GERMS

To relieve the pain of a sore throat caused by a cold, mix together ¼ cup of honey and ¼ cup of cider vinegar. Take 1 tablespoon every 4 hours. This remedy may be taken more often if needed.

Ease the discomfort of a sore throat and speed healing by sipping occasionally on a syrup made of ½ cup of cider vinegar, ½ cup of water, 1 teaspoon of cayenne pepper, and 3 tablespoons of honey.

• A vinegar gargle can ease the pain of a sore throat. Just gargle with a glass of warm water to which a tablespoon of cider vinegar has been added. Repeat as necessary. This also acts as a great mouthwash!

Soothe a dry cough at night by sprinkling the pillowcase with cider vinegar.

A small amount of vinegar, taken every day, keeps the urinary tract acidic. This reduces the likelihood of getting a kidney or bladder infection.

To chase away a cold, soak an eight-inch square of brown paper (cut from a paper bag) in cider vinegar. When the paper is saturated, sprinkle it with pepper and bind to the chest with cloth strips, pepper side of the paper next to the skin. After 20 minutes, remove the paper and wash the chest.

LOOK BETTER, FEEL BETTER

The most marvellous tonic for the feet is to walk back and forth in ankle deep bath water to which ½ a cup of cider vinegar has been added. Do this for 5 minutes first thing in the morning, and for 5 minutes before going to bed in the evening. Hot, aching feet will feel cooled and soothed.

If troubled by the itching and peeling of athlete's foot, soak your socks or tights in vinegar water. Mix 1 part vinegar with 5 parts water and soak for 30 minutes before washing as usual.

You can keep a full head of healthy, richly-coloured hair well into old age. You need only to start each day with a glass of water to which has been added 4 teaspoons each of cider vinegar, black treacle, and honey.

Cider vinegar is helpful in melting away excess pounds. Simply drink glass of warm water, with a single teaspoon of cider vinegar stirred in, before each meal. It reduces the appetite and melts away fat.

Whether vinegar actually burns up fatty calories, reduces the appetite, or simply makes you feel full, the results are the same. You eat less and the pounds melt away!

Asthma can be relieved by combining the advantages of accupressure with the benefits of cider vinegar. Use a wide rubber band to hold gauze pads, which have been soaked in vinegar, to the inside of the wrists.

You can banish dandruff and make hair shiny and healthy if you rinse after every shampoo with a half cup cider vinegar mixed into two cups of warm water.

- Use a vinegar and water rinse to eliminate frizz from hair that has been permed too often. It also brightens dark hair and adds sparkle to blond hair.

Ensure soft, radiant skin and prevent blemishes by conditioning the skin while sleeping with a covering of strawberries and vinegar. Mash 3 large strawberries into a ¼ cup of vinegar and let it sit for 2 hours. Then strain the vinegar through a cloth. Pat the strawberry flavoured vinegar onto the face and neck. Wash off in the morning. your skin will soon be free of pimples and blackheads.

Corns and calluses will fall away, overnight, if you treat them with a vinegar compress. Simply tape half a slice of stale bread which has been soaked with cider vinegar, to the offending lump. By morning the skin will look smooth and new.

Women can protect their skin from the ravages of the summer sun by applying a protective layer of olive oil and cider vinegar. Mixed half and half, this combination helps prevent sunburn and dry skin.

Liver spots (also called age spots) can be removed if you wipe them daily with onion juice and vinegar. One teaspoon of onion juice and 2 teaspoons of vinegar should be mixed together and applied with a soft cloth. Or, half a fresh onion can be dipped into a small dish of vinegar and then rubbed across the marked area of skin. In a few weeks the spot will begin to fade.

- Itchy swellings and blemishes of the skin can be eased by applying a paste made from vinegar and cornflour. Just pat it on to the affected area and feel the itch being drawn out as the paste dries.

Relieve uncomfortable and unsightly varicose veins by wrapping the legs with a cloth which has been dipped in cider vinegar and then wrung dry. Leave this on, with the legs propped up, for 30 minutes, morning and evening. Considerable relief will be noticed within 6 weeks. To speed up the healing process, follow each treatment with a glass of warm water to which a teaspoon of cider vinegar has been added. Sip slowly, and add a teaspoon of honey if you are feeling overtired.

● Another remedy for varicose veins is to apply undiluted cider vinegar to the affected veins twice a day, in the morning and evening. You should also drink two teaspoons of vinegar in a glass of water twice a day. After a month of this treatment the veins should have begun to shrink.

EASE PAIN & SUFFERING

Headaches will fade away if you follow this simple procedure: add a dash of cider vinegar to the water in a vaporiser and inhale the vapours for 5 minutes. Lay quietly and the headache should be relieved in 20 minutes.

Hiccups will disappear if you sip, very slowly, a glass of warm water with 1 teaspoon of vinegar in it. This works even better if you sip from the far side of the glass!

● Another cure for hiccups (which requires two people) is to sip a teaspoon of cider vinegar very slowly while plugging your ears with your fingers.

An unsettled stomach will be settled if you sip quietly on a glass of very warm water, to which has been added 1 tablespoon honey and 1 tablespoon vinegar. This is also good for easing flatulence.

If a headache will not go away, try a paper bag hat. Soak the bottom of the open edges of a brown paper bag in cider vinegar. Put the bag on the head (like a chef's hat) and tie it in place with a long scarf. The headache should be relieved in 45 minutes.

● Those plagued with night-time cramps in the legs can find relief by supplementing meals with a glass of water, fortified with cider vinegar.

Prevent leg cramps by combining 1 teaspoon of honey, 1 teaspoon of cider vinegar, and 1 tablespoon of calcium lactate in a half glass of water. This should be taken once a day.

Soothe tired or sprained muscles by wrapping the affected area with a cloth which has been dipped in cider vinegar and then wrung dry. Leave it on for 3 to 5 minutes and repeat as needed. For extra special relief, add a good dash of cayenne pepper to the vinegar.

Banish nausea or vomiting by placing a cloth which has been dipped in warm cider vinegar and then wrung dry on the stomach. Replace with another warm cloth when it cools.

Chapter Two

Vinegar Fights Disease

Cider vinegar enthusiasts can recite a long list of ailments it is reported to be able to cure or prevent. It is claimed vinegar can banish arthritis, forestall osteoporosis, prevent cancer, kill infections, improve the condition of the skin, aid digestion, control weight, preserve the memory, and prevent the mind from ageing.

On the pages which follow, some of the most recent findings of medical researchers, and the way this research affects vinegar therapy, are recorded. This chapter also includes some of the more enduring traditional remedies.

Can cider vinegar possibly do all that is claimed for it? One answer may be: 'Yes, because it is such a marvellous combination of sharp good taste and germ-killing acids.' Vinegar is fermented from apple juice, and takes its golden colour from tannins which flow from the ruptured cell walls of the fresh, ripe apples. When these naturally occurring colourless preservatives come into contact with air they develop the golden colour we associate with cider. This is called enzymatic browning. It contributes to the distinctive flavour of cider, a flavour with more bite than simple apple juice.

• Cider vinegar is made when fresh, naturally sweet apple juice is fermented into the alcoholic drink cider. Then it is fermented once again. The result is vinegar.

Cider vinegar contains more than thirty important nutrients, a dozen minerals, over half a dozen vitamins and essential acids, and several enzymes. Plus, it has a large dose of pectin for a healthy heart.

When cider vinegar is exposed to heat and air, it gives off some hints of its character. Take a healthy sniff and what you inhale is the 'volatile' part of vinegar — the portion which evaporates easily. Scientists recently analysed this smell. They found they were able to recognise 93 different volatile components, in addition there were others yet to be classified!

Vinegar has:
7 Hydrocarbons
18 Alcohols
33 Carbonyls (4 aldehydes and 29 ketones)
4 Acids
8 Esters (plus 11 lactone esters)
7 Bases
3 Furans
13 Phenols

The exact composition of a particular vinegar depends on what it was made from. Even cider vinegar varies with the kind and condition of the apples in it. Partly because of this, scientists do not always know exactly how or why it promotes healing. They do know it is both an antiseptic and an antibiotic.

VINEGAR'S EARLIEST MEDICAL USES

One of the earliest references to vinegar is in an early Assyrian medical text describing the application of vinegar to treat earache.

- In 400 BC, Hippocrates (considered the father of medicine) used vinegar to treat his patients. This naturally occurring germ killer was one of the very first 'medicines'.

- Vinegar was used as a healing dressing on wounds and infectious sores in Biblical times.

- 'Thieves Vinegar' got its name during the time of the Great Plague. Some enterprising thieves are said to have used cloths soaked in vinegar held over the mouth and nose to protect them from contamination while they robbed the homes of plague victims.

- Vinegar is credited with saving the lives of thousands of soldiers during the American Civil War. It was routinely used as a disinfectant on wounds.

VINEGAR AND THE SKIN

Throughout history, infections on the face, around the eyes, and in the ears have been treated with a solution of vinegar and water. It works because vinegar is antiseptic (it kills germs on contact) and antibiotic (it contains bacteria which are unfriendly to infectious micro-organisms).

More recently, vinegar has been used to treat chronic middle ear diseases when traditional drug-based methods fail. One treatment currently being used for ear infections is irrigation with vinegar.

Doctors are currently considering the possibility of treating some eye infections with diluted vinegar. It is also used as a hospital disinfectant. One example of this use is at Yale-New Haven Hospital in America. When post-surgery eye infections became a problem, their Department of Bacteriology solved the problem with vinegar. The hospital began routinely cleaning the scrub-room sink with a 0.5% solution of ordinary household vinegar. They found it worked better at eliminating the offending bacteria than any commercial product!

Vinegar And Beauty

For many people the smell of cider vinegar, and its association with food, makes them reluctant to use it as a beauty treatment. You can avoid this problem if you prepare the following lotion. Put half a pint (300ml) of rain water in a pan and add 1½oz (40g) of fresh rosemary. Bring to the boil, then simmer for 15 minutes, strain and add half a pint (300ml) of cider vinegar. Cool and bottle.

The lotion can be used on the hair, either as a conditioner rubbed into the scalp, or as a final rinse. In both cases it acts to restore the natural pH balance of the scalp (the scalp is slightly acid, while most shampoos are alkaline).

It can also be used on the skin, dabbing it gently into wrinkles.

● Regular users of cider vinegar often notice that the whites of their eyes are particularly bright and clear.

Vinegar And Burns

Two traditional remedies for treating mild burns were to douse the burn with cider vinegar or to let a snail crawl over it. If you don't have a tame snail you may want to try dabbing cider vinegar onto a painful burn. Vinegar is particularly useful for neutralising burns caused by alkalis, like oven cleaners for example.

Cool sunburn by soaking in a bath of lukewarm water, to which a cup of cider vinegar has been added. Whenever a sprain or ache needs to be soaked in very hot water, a splash of vinegar in the water will make it seem cooler.

- Those who regularly consume vinegar feel that it helps cuts and abrasions heal faster, as well as speeding up the healing of more serious wounds.

Vinegar And Impetigo

Impetigo is a highly infectious skin disease, caused by the staphylococcus or streptococcus bacteria. The skin blisters and is covered in a yellow crust. To treat impetigo with cider vinegar apply it undiluted direct to the affected areas of the skin using your finger (don't use a cloth). Repeat the treatment six times a day. The impetigo should clear up within a few days.

- One reason vinegar is so very helpful in treating skin disorders is that it has a pH which is nearly the same as healthy skin. So, applying vinegar helps to normalise the pH of the skin's surface.

Vinegar And Itching

Itchy skin can be relieved by patting on cider vinegar. If the itch is near the eyes or other delicate areas, dilute the vinegar, 1 part vinegar to 4 parts water. For a full body treatment, put 2 or 3 cups of vinegar in the bath water. A handful of thyme can help too.

Dampen a gauze square in cider vinegar and apply, gently, to ease rectal itching.

Vinegar And Ringworm

Ringworm is a skin condition caused by a fungus. The usual site of the infection is the head. The fungus causes small round patches on the scalp where the hair breaks off near the root, there may be inflammation of the skin in the area. The fungus is most common in male children.

To treat ringworm with cider vinegar apply it undiluted direct to the affected areas of the skin using your fingers. Repeat the treatment six times a day.

- Use a cloth moistened in vinegar to clean your armpits. Do not rinse it off — it will eliminate offensive odours for several hours.

VINEGAR, FIBRE AND CHOLESTEROL

Vinegar contains a wealth of complex carbohydrates, as well as a good dose of that mysterious stuff called 'dietary fibre'. Both complex carbohydrates and dietary fibre are recommended to help reduce the risk of developing cancer.

- There are different kinds of dietary fibres. Some are water soluble and some are not. Water soluble fibre soaks up water (adding bulk) and also interacts with the body. Insoluble fibres soak up water (adding bulk) but do not interact with the body in the same complex way soluble fibres do.

When vinegar is made from fresh, natural apples it contains a healthy dose of pectin. Pectin is a soluble fibre. It dissolves in water, making it available for the body to use. In addition to soaking up water, it slows down the absorption of food and liquid in the intestines. Therefore, it stays in the body longer than an insoluble fibre.

- An insoluble fibre, like bran, rushes through the system, particularly, through the intestines. This gives it laxative properties. Bran may also produce large amounts of flatulence.

As pectin (cider vinegar fibre) works its slow, gentle way through the digestive system it binds to cholesterol. Then it takes the cholesterol which is bound to it out of the body. Less cholesterol in the body makes for a reduced risk of cardiovascular problems, for example heart attacks and strokes.

VINEGAR AND DIGESTION

Cider vinegar is very similar to chemicals found naturally in the stomach. Because of this, it has traditionally been considered an aid to digestion. And so, by improving digestion, it is felt it will improve the overall metabolism of the body.

Vinegar is considered by many to be able to attack and kill harmful bacteria which have invaded the digestive tract. This may lessen the likelihood of the body developing toxaemia and other blood-borne infections.

- Cider vinegar definitely has a beneficial effect on digestion. It aids the process in a number of ways. In the mouth it makes the saliva slightly acid, and this helps the enzymes which act to break down food. In the small intestine it seems to aid the bacteria that help to break down food, while the potassium and acetic acid it contains gets rid of harmful bacteria.

Vinegar And Diarrhoea

Cider vinegar can be used as a 'first aid' treatment for diarrhoea. Drink three or four pints of water a day adding a teaspoon of cider vinegar to each half pint. This soon deals with the problem.

Vinegar And Food Poisoning

Some doctors suggest using vinegar regularly to prevent food poisoning. They recommend its use when food hygiene may be doubtful. The usual dose is to take 1 tablespoon of vinegar, 30 minutes before meals. It can be mixed with a glass of water, vegetable juice, or any other drink. Honey added to vinegar and water makes the taste more palatable for most people.

- A vinegar experiment anyone can try is to use it to make pulses more digestible, and so less likely to produce flatulence. Just splash a little vinegar in the pot when cooking dried beans. It will make them tender and easy to digest.

Vinegar And Indigestion

Many people find that drinking a glass of water to which a teaspoon of cider vinegar has been added prevents indigestion and flatulence. They take the drink with each meal.

VINEGAR AND SLIMMING

Most diets only work for a short period of time. The slimmer loses weight rapidly, then gradually returns to their old ways of eating. The result is a cycle of overeating followed by dieting which is unhealthy and not much fun!

Cider vinegar can play a part in changing the whole way that you eat. The result is a slow but steady weight loss, until you reach your correct weight. Then, since you've retrained yourself to eat properly, you stay at that weight. Also, the new way of eating is good for you, so most people find that their general health is better.

To slim with cider vinegar you must first improve the quality of your diet. Take a realistic look at the way you eat at the moment. You should be eating some green vegetables and fruit every day, along with some protein. You should be eating wholemeal bread and using wholemeal flour in cooking where you can. Most people eat too much salt, fat, and sugar. Is this true of you? If you eat any quantity of convenience or snack foods it's likely to be. Try to reduce your salt and sugar intake. Reduce the amount of fat you eat by 10%. Substitute some dairy fats with vegetable oils that are high in polyunsaturates.

- Start the day with a glass of water containing two teaspoons of cider vinegar. Prepare the drink before you go to bed, and drink it before you get up in the morning.

- Drink a glass of water containing two teaspoons of cider vinegar with each meal. Drink it slowly so that it lasts for the whole meal. The idea is that it should affect the way you digest the food. With this in mind, make sure that you chew your food thoroughly to give the enzymes in your mouth time to act on it before you swallow.

By combining your improved diet with cider vinegar you should find that you gradually lose weight. It won't happen overnight, but the weight that comes off will stay off!

VINEGAR, BETA CAROTENE, AND CANCER

Ageing, heart disease, cancer, and cataracts are symptoms of the harm done to the human body by free radicals, the 'loose cannons' of the cell world. They damage chromosomes and are probably responsible for many of the physical changes associated with ageing.

Free radicals roam through plants, animals, and humans, bouncing from cell to cell, damaging each in turn. Antioxidants absorb free radicals, making them harmless. Beta carotene, found in vinegar, is a powerful antioxidant.

Beta carotene occurs naturally in fruits like apples. Vinegar's beta carotene is in a natural, easy-to-digest form. One example of how this antioxidant contributes to maintaining good health is the way it protects the eye from cataracts. Cataract development is related to oxidation of the eye's lens. This happens when free radicals alter its structure. Studies show that eating large amounts of antioxidant-containing foods decreases the risk of forming cataracts.

A correlation between eating foods containing beta carotene and a lower risk of cancer has also been documented. Researchers in more than 70 different studies agree that beta carotene reduces the risk of developing cancer. They include those at the University of Western Ontario in Canada and the State University of New York, Tufts University, and Johns Hopkins School of Medicine in America.

- In addition to giving cancer protection, beta carotene boosts the body's immune system. It works by attacking the free radicals which damage the immune system.

Beta carotene is also the body's raw material for producing vitamin A, another potent antioxidant. They act together to give protection from cancers associated with chemical toxins. According to the National Cancer Research Centre, when the body does not get enough vitamin A, it is particularly susceptible to cancers of the respiratory system, bladder and colon.

- Traditional remedies have long recommended taking a teaspoon of vinegar, every day, in a glass of vegetable juice. With all we now know about fibre and beta carotene, this may turn out to be very good advice!

VINEGAR AND MEMORY

Memory loss is one of the most common and costly diseases of the elderly. The cost of memory loss in disrupted lives, and reduced quality of life is enormous. And this is true not just for those suffering from memory loss. but often for their loved ones as well.

The three most common causes of memory loss are: Alzheimer's disease, multiple strokes (multi-infarct dementia) and alcohol abuse. Many other elderly people endure mental impairment caused by poor nutrition and reactions to prescription drugs.

Too often memory loss in individuals who are over 55 is treated as if it were irreversible or inevitable. Yet, information continues to pile up which proves memory loss can be successfully treated. More and more doctors are echoing the words of one specialist:

'. . . *several of the causes are treatable, resulting in an arrest or actual reversal of the symptoms.'*

Diet is an important factor in control of risk factors for memory loss, and in reversing damage which has already been done. Good nutrition can decrease the likelihood of a stroke by lowering cholesterol levels. It can also protect the mind from some of the worse causes of loss of mental function. The Journal of the American Dietetic Association puts it this way:

'Some forms of dementia — those due to excessive alcohol intake or vitamin deficiency — may be entirely preventable and partially reversible through diet.'

Dementia which is associated with excessive alcohol intake is particularly treatable. The Journal goes on to say:

'In all types of dementia, adequate nutrition may improve physical well-being, help maximise the patients' functioning, and improve the quality of life.'

Some studies indicate nutritional deficiencies are a problem for 36% of the population aged over 80. And nearly half of all nursing home patients have been shown to have some vitamin or mineral deficiency. These lower than normal levels of vitamins and minerals are important because they contribute to loss of mental ability. For example, memory loss is more frequent in patients who have lower than normal blood levels of vitamin B_{12} and folic acid.

- Cider vinegar supplies a balanced dose of vital amino acids, vitamins, and minerals that both the mind and body need for good health.

The worst of the mind robbing diseases associated with ageing is Alzheimer's disease (AD). Some studies show AD sufferers are particularly short of calcium, thiamine (vitamin B_1) and niacin. And low B_{12} levels have been reported in up to 30% of elderly patients with this kind of dementia. Almost every patient in a recent study of nutrient deficiencies showed complete recovery when given vitamin B_{12} therapy. Folic acid supplements also proved valuable.

Thiamine deficiency is another nutritional cause of chronic memory problems. If the diet is sufficiently short of this nutrient, nerve cell loss and haemorrhages in the brain can result. Experts continue to remind us:

'. . . dietary modification may play an important role in the control of several diseases that may produce a dementia.'

The more we learn about good nutrition and the importance of getting an assortment of vitamins and minerals each day, the easier it is to understand the use of cider vinegar in traditional remedies. One grandmother suggests this way to a healthy old age:

'Stir a teaspoon of cider vinegar and a teaspoon of honey into a glass of water and drink it with your meal. Do this 3 times a day to remain bright and alert all your life.'

Treating malnutrition with megadoses of vitamins is being tested, with mixed results. Sometimes it is difficult to get the balanced dose a particular individual may need. And, there is always the possibility of doing harm by giving too many vitamins, or of giving an overdose of minerals. Vitamin therapy can also be expensive.

● It is much better to prevent nutrient shortages by eating a balanced diet. And, for balancing the diet, it is hard to match the variety of vitamins and minerals contained in a tablespoon of cider vinegar.

VINEGAR AND ARTHRITIS

Each year large sums of money and resources are spent trying to find relief for arthritis sufferers — relief that, too often, does not come. Those who are suffering the pain of arthritis will try almost anything to be free of the disease. This often results in large sums of money being spent on supposed cures which do not improve health, relieve chronic pain, or stop the progression of the disease.

The Journal of the American Dietetic Association notes that both medical and nutrition authorities agree on one important fact about arthritis care:

The only specific treatment for arthritis is 'Weight control . . . and a nutrient-dense diet . . .'

This renowned journal goes on to explain the conclusions nutritional scientists have drawn from studies of the eating habits of arthritis sufferers:

Sometimes the patient's diet is found to be '. . . grossly deficient in some nutrients.'

Perhaps this helps to explain the long-standing belief by many that cider vinegar can play an important part in relieving the pain and slowing the progression of arthritis. At the very least it is less likely to harm the person taking it than some of the more outrageous chemicals which have been advertised as being able to ease the symptoms of arthritis. And, in addition, it is inexpensive!

- The time-honoured vinegar recipe for dealing with arthritis is 1 teaspoon of honey and 1 teaspoon of cider vinegar, mixed into a glass of water and taken morning and evening.

Another recommended treatment for arthritis is to take two teaspoons of cider vinegar, two of black treacle, and one of honey in a glass of water with each meal. Sufferers should also eat a diet which is low in sugar, white flour and animal fat, and take a daily vitamin and mineral supplement.

Others believe the proper dose is to drink a glass of water, with 2 teaspoons of vinegar in it, 3 times a day before meals.

Another tonic which has often been recommended for those who suffer from the pain of arthritis includes vinegar with celery, Epsom salts, and citrus fruits (for vitamin C). Combine in a saucepan:

½ a grapefruit
1 orange
1 lemon
2 stalks of celery
4 cups of water

Cut the celery and fruit (including the peelings) into chunks. Simmer in water, uncovered, for 1 hour. Press the softened foods through a strainer and then stir in 1 tablespoon vinegar and 1 tablespoon of Epsom salts. Drink a full glass of water, morning and evening, to which ¼ cup of this tonic has been added.

With any of these vinegar regimes, expect it to take about a month for relief to begin. For more immediate results, many doctors says a gentle rubdown may help. One traditional liniment combines vinegar and oil with egg whites:

31

2 egg whites
½ cup of turpentine*
½ cup of vinegar
¼ cup of olive oil

Mix all the ingredients together and use right away. Gently massage aching joints with this mixture, then wipe it off with a soft cloth.

*Most medical authorities would recommend leaving the turpentine out of this remedy, as it can cause skin irritation.

VINEGAR AND IRON

Children, adolescents and adult women of child-bearing age should be sure to consume generous amounts of foods that are high in iron. Iron deficiency is a special problem for low-income families.

● Others who should be sure they are getting lots of iron in their diets are frequent users of aspirin. Aspirin often causes intestinal blood loss, putting the user at risk of iron deficiency

One long-standing solution to low iron intake is to cook in iron pots. Each time one of these pans is used, some iron leaches into food. The higher the acid content of foods, the more iron will be absorbed into food. Adding a splash of vinegar to meats, sauces, and stews will raise their acid content. This increases the amount of iron they leach from iron pans.

To prevent anaemia, the body needs iron, vitamin B_{12}, folic acid and a wide range of other nutrients. Cider vinegar delivers many of these nutrients in an easy to digest and absorb form.

VINEGAR AND CALCIUM

Calcium is the most abundant mineral in the human body. Besides its well-known part in forming bones, calcium is necessary for many other parts of the body to work properly. Although only 1% of the body's calcium is found outside the skeleton, without this small amount muscles do not contract properly, blood clotting is affected, and the working of the nervous system is seriously impaired.

Calcium absorption is affected by the amount of certain other substances in the body. For example, a diet too rich in phosphorus can cause calcium not to be absorbed properly. Or, eating too much protein can interfere with calcium absorption. Then, even if enough calcium is eaten, the body cannot draw it out of food and use it.

Each year thousands of women suffer fractured hips. Two thirds of these women will never return to normal life. Nearly 15% will die within six months of the fractures, from complications. Others find their spinal column begins to collapse, reducing height and producing the back deformity known as a widow's hump. Osteoporosis is a major factor in these disabling fractures.

- As the body ages it is less and less efficient at extracting calcium from food. Adding to this is the fact that with age, people tend to consume less and less calcium. Some of this is because many older individuals develop lactose intolerance, causing them to drop calcium-rich dairy products from their diets.

So it comes as no surprise that many individuals find their bones begin to shrink as they get older. As osteoporosis advances, bones decrease in both size and density. The result is porous, fragile bones that fracture easily. It is a serious health problem, causing deformity, disability, and pain.

• Bones are living tissue. They are constantly being rebuilt and replaced. Whenever there is a shortage of calcium in muscles, blood, or nerves, the body pulls it from bones.

Cider vinegar contains a trace of much-needed calcium. It can also be used to dissolve calcium in soup bones. Several recent scientific reports show that when vinegar is added to the water in which soup bones are cooked, it leaches calcium from the bones and deposits it in the soup stock!

Some time-tested ways to combine vinegar and calcium, and some new ways validated by the latest medical research follow.

Chicken Soup

To make a delicious, low calorie, calcium-rich chicken soup you will need:
½ cup of vinegar
2-3lbs (1-1.5kg) of chicken bones
¾ cup of tiny pasta
2 stock cubes
2 slightly beaten egg whites
2 tablespoons of freshly chopped parsley

Begin with a gallon of water and at least ½ cup of vinegar. Gently simmer the chicken bones (chicken wings are a good choice) for about 2 hours, uncovered. Strain the broth and skim off all fat. Strip the meat from the bones and add the chicken, pasta, and stock cubes to the stock. Bring to a boil and cook for 10 minutes. Remove from heat and immediately dribble the egg whites into the hot liquid, stirring continuously. Mix in the parsley and serve. This soup is low in calories, healthy, and it adds calcium to the diet!

• As little as one tablespoon of vinegar per quart of water can make a difference to the amount of calcium which is extracted from boiled soup bones. A stronger vinegar solution (such as that used above) results in even more calcium being added to soup!

Another way to add calcium to the diet is to crumble feta cheese over torn greens. Use spinach and kale in addition to lettuce leaves. Sprinkle on a mixture of 2 tablespoons of cider vinegar, 2 tablespoons of honey, and 2 tablespoons of water.

The latest research describes calcium supplements as being useful in the prevention and treatment of osteoporosis. Calcium supplements are prescribed for those with calcium deficient diets, elderly people who do not metabolise calcium adequately, and for those with increased calcium needs (this can include post-menopausal women). This calcium is usually added to the diet by taking calcium tablets, or in the form of antacid tablets.

A calcium tablet should dissolve in a maximum time of 30 minutes. An antacid tablet should be completely broken down in 10 minutes. If a tablet takes longer to break up than the recommended time, its usefulness is seriously impaired.

Studies estimate that more than half of the popular calcium supplements on the market do not dissolve in these times. Yet, calcium supplements can only be properly used by the body if they disintegrate in a reasonable length of time after being taken.

A simple-to-use vinegar test can tell you whether or not your calcium supplement dissolves in time for your body to digest it properly:

1   Drop the calcium supplement tablet into three fluid ounces of room temperature vinegar.

2   Stir briskly, once every five minutes.

At the end of 30 minutes the tablet should be completely disintegrated.

Tests by medical researchers found that times varied widely among the most popular brands. One brand of calcium supplement tablet broke up completely in three minutes. Another popular tablet was still mostly intact after 30 minutes.

3 to 4 million people in this country are affected by osteoporosis. This contributes to the thousands of bone fractures, every year that occur to individuals over 45 years old. Over the years, this adds up to a lot of disability. For example, one out of every three women over 65 has at least one fractured vertebra. When these tiny back bones crack, they can cause disabling pain.

Hip fractures are an even bigger problem. By 90 years of age, one out of every six men and one out of every three women will have suffered a fractured hip. One out of each five hip fractures leads to death. Long term nursing care is required for many others.

As the body ages, the stomach produces less acid. Some believe this fact contributes to calcium shortages in elderly people. After all, acid is needed to dissolve almost all calcium supplement tablets. One solution may be to take calcium supplements with an old-fashioned vinegar tonic. It not only has acid for dissolving calcium, it adds the bit of extra calcium which is in vinegar!

VINEGAR AND BORON

Have you had your boron today? If you began the day with cider vinegar your body is probably well fortified against boron deficiency. This vital trace element is needed for good health and strong bones.

Boron is a mineral which is necessary for both plant and animal life. When it is not readily available to plants, they do not grow properly. Some become dwarfs and others crack and become disfigured. The human body does not make strong, straight bones when boron is missing from the diet. One reason for this is that it plays a critical role in the way the body uses calcium. Without boron, calcium cannot form and maintain strong bones.

When vinegar releases its boron into the body, all sorts of wonderfully healthy things begin to happen. Boron affects the way steroid hormones are released. Then it regulates both their use and how long they stay active in the body.

• How boron builds bones is only now beginning to be understood by scientists. One of the few things they do know is it makes changes in the way the membrane around individual cells works.

The boron and hormone connection is vital to bone formation. Blood and tissue levels of several steroid hormones (such as oestrogen and testosterone) increase dramatically in the presence of boron. Both of these are needed to complete the calcium-to-bone growth cycle. This relationship between hormones, boron, and calcium helps to explain why oestrogen replacement is about the only treatment for osteoporosis.

Some other trace elements necessary for maintaining bone mass are manganese, silicon, and magnesium. Some doctors recommend supplements of all of them for post-menopausal women, even though no one knows exactly how they work. Many feel boron is useful for treating a lot of the ailments (such as arthritis) that doctors are not able to treat with great success with drugs.

We do know that cider vinegar supplies boron, as well as manganese, silicon, and magnesium to the body. Even more importantly, it does so in a natural, balanced way.

VINEGAR AND OTHER AILMENTS

There are traditional vinegar treatments for a host of other ailments. Here are a selection of some of the most well-use and successful

Angina

Some sufferers from angina (heart pain) have found that taking a regular treatment of cider vinegar reduced the pain of angina attacks. Take two teaspoons in a glass of water three times a day.

Chronic fatigue

If you suffer from an almost permanent feeling of fatigue and general tiredness, try this traditional treatment.

Take half a glass of warm water, and add a teaspoon of cider vinegar. Pour about a teaspoon of the mixture into the palm of your hand, and rub it into your arm and shoulder. Repeat with the other arm and shoulder, and then the rest of your body in the following order: chest, stomach, back, upper leg, lower leg, feet. Don't dry yourself with a towel, let the mixture soak into your skin.

Repeat this treatment whenever you feel particularly tired.

Dizziness

If you suffer frequent bouts of dizziness, whether short or long-lasting, you can treat yourself with cider vinegar. Take two teaspoons in a glass of water twice a day for two weeks. You should find that your dizziness had decreased. If not, continue treatment for another two weeks.

Weak Fingernails

People, particularly older people, who suffer from brittle, thin or weak nails often find that this problem is greatly reduced, or goes away all together if they regularly consume cider vinegar. The treatment may take some time — anything up to a year — but in most people a marked improvement can be seen.

• From time to time most people's nails are marked with white spots. These are usually associated with a lack of calcium. It has often been noted that these spots disappear when cider vinegar is taken regularly. This is another sign of the way in which vinegar helps the body absorb calcium (see Vinegar and Calcium, page 33 for more details).

Hay Fever and Asthma

Hay fever is caused by an excessive sensitivity to foreign proteins. A sufferer breaths these proteins in and reacts to them, causing the familiar symptoms of runny nose, watering eyes, sneezing and so on. It is well documented that many suffers have found a mixture of cider vinegar and honey brings relief. In some cases it may give a complete cure.

The normal treatment is to take two teaspoons of honey with two teaspoons of cider vinegar in a glass of warm water once a day through out the season. Some sufferers recommend taking this all year round.

This same treatment, taken three times a day has also proved effective for asthma. However it is important that at the same time as taking the treatment you try and remove from your life as many of the factors that trigger an attack as possible.

Many sufferers also find that there is a direct relationship between obesity and the number of attacks. If you are a bit overweight, slimming down may improve your asthma. See the section on Vinegar And Slimming for more advice (page 25).

- Catarrh can be relived by heating cider vinegar in a saucepan (not aluminium or copper), then breathing in the vapours for five or ten minutes.

Insomnia

Cider vinegar can form part of a restful relaxation routine that will get you into the right frame of mind for good nights sleep — this is the best way to deal with insomnia.

Just before you go to bed drink a glass or warm water containing two teaspoons of cider vinegar and two teaspoons of honey. Lie on the bed and relax your whole body and fill your mind with pleasant thoughts.

Sore Mouth and gums

A cider vinegar mouthwash can be an effective treatment for mouth ulcers, sores, and bleeding gums. However don't repeat the treatment too often, latest research suggests that over-frequent application of vinegar may damage tooth enamel (see page 104).

Rheumatism

Rheumatism is a popular name for a condition in which the muscles become stiff and painful. It is thought that this may be caused by a build up of toxins within the muscles themselves. Many sufferers have found relief by taking a mixture of two teaspoons of cider vinegar, two of black treacle, and one of honey in a glass of water with each meal.

Shingles

Cider vinegar, applied direct to the skin, can often bring relief from the pain of shingles. The affected area should be dabbed with undiluted cider vinegar until the pain starts to ease. Repeat the treatment every one or two hours.

Sore throat

A sore throat may be treated with cider vinegar, as the bacteria that often cause sore throats prefer an alkali environment. Drink half a glass of water containing one teaspoon of cider vinegar. Repeat this every hour for the next six or seven hours

Or you may like to try a cider vinegar gargle. Heat half a pint (300ml) of cider vinegar, and add 1oz (25g) of red sage, ½oz (12g) of self-heal (Prunella Vulgaris), and 4oz (100g) of honey. Do not allow the vinegar to boil, cool the mixture and set aside for twenty four hours. Strain the mixture. When you have a sore throat gargle with two teaspoons of the mixture in half a glass of water.

• A cough can often be relieved by sipping at a glass of water containing four teaspoons of cider vinegar.

JAPANESE RICE VINEGAR AND HEALTH

Taking vinegar and honey as a life enhancing tonic is more than just a Western custom. In Japan it is an old favourite, too.

Japan's most famous vinegar is made from rice. The bulk of Japanese commercial vinegar is made from wine leftovers. The sediment left from the production of the rice wine called 'sake' is used to make industrial vinegar. These dregs, called 'lees' produce a vinegar which is similar in nutrient value to our white vinegar.

The rice vinegar which is used for cooking and healing remedies is made directly from brown rice. Belief in the healing properties of this deeply coloured rice vinegar has come down through thousands of years of Japanese culture.

Some ways of using vinegar that have endured for centuries — and some of Japan's newest research into the healing power of rice vinegar follow:

According to the Japan Food Research Laboratories, vinegar made directly from brown rice has five times the amount of amino acids as the commercial product made from lees. Perhaps the health-giving benefits of rice vinegar are because of the 20 amino acids it contains. Or maybe it is the 16 organic acids which can be found in it.

- The bottom of the bottle of even the best rice vinegar will have a fine rice sediment. When these grounds are disturbed they give the vinegar a muddy appearance. This dark residue is considered to be the mark of a high quality rice vinegar.

Recent research by Dr. Yoshio Takino, of Shizuka University in Japan, proved vinegar helps to maintain good health and slow down ageing by helping to prevent the formation of two fatty peroxides. This is important to good health and long life in two important ways. One is associated with damaging free radicals. The other with the cholesterol formations which build up on blood vessel walls.

In Japan, vinegar is used to produce one of that country's most potent folk remedies. Tamago-su or egg vinegar, is made by immersing a whole raw egg in a cup of rice vinegar. The egg and vinegar are left, undisturbed, for seven days. During this time the vinegar dissolves the egg, shell and all.

At the end of one week the only part of the egg which has not been dissolved is the transparent membrane, located just inside the shell. The Tamago-su maker splits open this membrane and dumps its contents into the glass of vinegar. This piece of the egg is discarded and what remains is thoroughly mixed.

A small amount of this very powerful egg vinegar is taken three times a day, stirred into a glass of hot water. It is believed it will assure a long, healthy life. Traditionally, Samurai warriors considered egg vinegar tonic to be an important source of strength and power.

Vinegar is used as a bleaching agent on white vegetables. It also prevents enzymatic browning. When foods do not darken in air, they do not develop the off-taste associated with browning. Rice vinegar is also used in salad dressings, marinades, sauces, dips, and spreads.

Rice vinegar (like all vinegars) is a powerful antiseptic. It kills, on contact, dangerous bacteria such as salmonella and streptococcus.

The sushi industry is largely dependent on vinegar's ability to prevent germs from growing on the raw fish. It is sprinkled on the fish, included in dipping sauces, and used as a preservative.

● Vinegar acts as a tenderiser on meats and vegetables used in stir-fry dishes.

Japanese housewives add a little rice vinegar to summer rice to prevent it from spoiling. Vinegar, added to fish dishes, helps to eliminate the traditional fishy odour. It also helps get rid of fish smells at washing up time.

Chapter Three

Where Did Vinegar Come From?

- 3,000 years before barley is grown to make beer.

- 4,000 years before all of Mesopotamia is engulfed in a disastrous flood.

- 5,000 years before wheeled vehicles appear in Sumeria or the Egyptians learn to plough.

An enterprising person prepares some fresh fruit juice and seals it tightly in a stone jar. In a short time it ferments into the mildly alcoholic drink we call wine.

Some time later a very special day follows. Wine is left open to the air. A second fermentation takes place. Vinegar is created!

Imagine the surprise of the poor soul who took the first sip of this new brew. All the alcohol in the wine had turned into a sharp tasting acid! Had a partially filled wine cask been unknowingly set aside and left uncared for? Had a servant carelessly left the wine uncorked? Or could it possibly be . . . did someone suspect the possibilities?

No one knows for sure how it happened, but vinegar entered the world. And the event was momentous! Vinegar was found to be an almost universal preservative and cure-all. Vegetables submerged in this wonderful liquid kept their fresh colour and crispness. Fish remained edible long after they should have rotted. Festering sores, when doused with it, began to heal. It is not surprising that mankind would hold this amazing concoction in high esteem.

- Our word 'vinegar' comes from the French 'vinaigre' — VIN (wine) and AIGRE (sour). And that is just what it is — wine that has gone sour.

Although vinegar can be made from almost any mildly sweet liquid, the most miraculous claims for health benefits are linked to vinegar made from cider. So, unless literature specifically says otherwise, references to vinegar in instructions for healing usually mean cider vinegar.

- Cider has been made in Britain for thousands of years. It is thought that there were cultivated orchards in Neolithic times. Apples are native to Britain — they are one of the few fruits that have moved from east to west over time.

Once the ancient world recognised vinegar's value for healing and health, the intentional production of this amazing elixir began. Because vinegar could do so many miraculous things it is not surprising that the souring of cider into vinegar was often an elaborate process, with overtones of magic.

- Vinegar making was, for thousands of years, more an art than a science. The physical steps for making vinegar were often augmented with incantations and seemingly superfluous steps.

We now know the complicated recipes of the mediaeval alchemists were not needed. These early recipes owed their success to the accidental infection of their brews with organisms needed for fermentation. It was this plus exposure to air which brought vinegar into being!

WHAT IS VINEGAR?

Technically, vinegar is an acid liquid made from wine, cider, beer (or almost any mildly alcoholic beverage) by what is called an 'acetous fermentation'. What this means, is that alcohol reacts with oxygen in the air. The alcohol then 'disappears'. (Actually, it is changed into acetic acid and water.)

Acetic acid is what imparts the characteristic tart taste to vinegar — the taste that makes you want to pucker you lips. The acetous fermentation which creates it is due to a tiny micro-organism, the vinegar bacillus. This bacterium occurs naturally in the air everywhere, and it is because of this that early vinegar producers were successful.

It was not until 1578, nearly 10,000 years after vinegar making began, that a microbiologist named Hansen correctly explained the chemical process which creates vinegar. He accurately described the three species of vinegar bacilli. These tiny creatures gobble up alcohol and excrete acid. The process where alcohols are changed to acids is called fermentation.

Fermenting is thought by many to give the end product a special ability to heal. It is also thought to sharply increase nutritional values. While the primary reason for pickling foods was, originally, to keep them from rotting, the result can be better tasting than the original — just ask any pickle fan.

Vinegar contains dilute acetic acid. It also has the basic nature and essential nutrients of the original food from which it was made. For example, cider vinegar has pectin, beta carotene, and potassium from the apples that it was made from. In addition, it contains generous portions of health-giving enzymes and amino acids. These complex protein building blocks are formed during the fermentation process.

Claims for the curative and restorative powers of cider vinegar are legendary. Some believe this fabulous liquid is capable of solving the most vexing and tiresome of human afflictions. It has been said to lengthen life and improve hearing, vision, and mental powers.

● Devotees claim it will help heartburn, clear up throat irritations, stop hiccups, relieve coughs, deal with diarrhoea, and ease asthma.

Over the centuries vinegar became a commonplace remedy for many ills. It was also found to be useful in cleaning, cooking, and food preservation. Some examples of ancient recipes for health, well-being and cleaning follow.

Ye may ease the rasping of the evening cough by sleeping with the head on a cloth which has been steeped in vinegar.

An aching throat will be eased by rinsing it with water which has been made to blush by the addition of vinegar.

Difficult breathing may be eased by wrapping strips of white cloth, well dampened with vinegar, around the wrists.

Ye may purify the waters of the body by sipping a tonic of goodly vinegar, mixed with clear running water. Those who sup regularly of the miraculous vinegar will be blessed with a sharp mind for all their life.

Bumps, lumps, and knots of the flesh may be relieved by the timely application of a binding soaked in the best vinegar.

Itching of the flesh may be relieved by the frequent application of vinegar.

Alleviate the discomfort of aching in the lower limbs by wrapping the afflicted area with a cloth wrung out of cider vinegar. When the binding begins to dry, renew it with fresh vinegar.

Make the suffering of one who speweth up their food less grievous by covering the belly with a well washed cloth, well soaked in warm vinegar.

Before scrubbing garments, sprinkle them with vinegar to make the task lighter. This will also make the fabric more agreeable.

Vinegar and salt added to washing water will drive bugs from garden foods.

Saddles and boots may be cleaned with beeswax, soap, oil, and vinegar. Carefully work beeswax into warm vinegar, then add soap and oil. Heat until the ingredients are thoroughly mixed and cool before using.

Soak venison (or other fresh flesh) in vinegar and water before cooking. This will make it palatable and soft for the teeth.

Coarse, sinewy vegetables become more toothsome if, before cooling, they are allowed to rest in water laced with vinegar.

HERB VINEGARS

The 'doctors' of the ancient world quickly learned to combine vinegar with particular plants for maximum medicinal value. Herb vinegars have been in use for thousands of years. Yet, the virtues of healing herbs are only now beginning to be understood by the scientific community. Some examples of vinegars considered to be both health-giving and antiseptic follow (see the Cooking With Vinegar chapter for directions on preparing herb vinegars):

DANDELION adds its mild laxative nature to vinegar's natural antiseptic qualities. It also has an anti-inflammatory effect on the intestines. This is a traditional remedy for ailments of the pancreas and liver, said to ease jaundice and cirrhosis. It is also a diuretic, and as such is considered useful in lowering blood pressure. (Dandelion is rich in potassium, a mineral some other diuretics pull out of the body.)

MYRRH has long been considered of particular value in maintaining a healthy mouth. Swish this vinegar around in the mouth to hasten healing of sores and to soothe red, swollen gums. This will also sweeten the breath. It was also used it for treating chest congestion.

SAGE vinegar not only adds its delicate hint of flavouring to meats, it tenderises them. Splashed into soups and dressings, it acts as a tranquilliser for frazzled nerves.

PEPPERMINT like all the mints, settles and calms the digestive system. Use a couple of teaspoons of peppermint vinegar, added to a glass of water, to ease stomach cramps, diarrhoea, or flatulence. Add a teaspoon of honey for one of the best tasting cures for indigestion. Mix this herb vinegar with others to intensify their flavour and effectiveness.

ROSEMARY the herb of remembrance, combines with healthy, amino acid laced cider vinegar to treat maladies of the head. It boosts the function of mind and memory, relieves tension headaches, and eases dizziness.

EUCALYPTUS is the source of the oil which makes some cough drops so effective. Steam from vinegar which has absorbed the aromatic oil of this herb helps to clear a stuffy head or a clogged respiratory system. A popular over-the counter cream for relieving the stiffness and swelling of arthritis and rheumatism carries the distinctive aroma of eucalyptus.

WORMWOOD is quite bitter. This vinegar is best used externally, as a deterrent to fleas and other insects, or applied as a wound dressing. For insect control, sprinkle it liberally onto infested areas of rooms.

RUE was once given as an antidote for poison mushrooms and toadstools, as well as the bite of snakes, spiders, and bees. Bitter, aromatic rue vinegar was once sprinkled about to ward off both witches and contagious diseases.

LAVENDER makes a vinegar that is pleasantly aromatic and useful for fighting off anxiety attacks. The haunting scent of lavender has long been associated with headache relief and calming of stressed nerves.

THYME vinegar is a good addition to meat dishes, as it both flavours and tenderises. Applied to the body, it acts to deter fungal growth.

SPEARMINT is one of the gentler mints. A bit of spearmint vinegar in a glass of water calms the stomach and digestive system. It also relieves indigestion and adds slangy zing to iced tea.

CLOVE vinegar is especially good for preventing vomiting. Its use dates back more than 2,000 years (to China) where it was considered an aphrodisiac.

- When herb vinegars are used for medicinal purposes, the usual dose is one to three teaspoons added to a full glass of water. They can also be sprinkled into meat and vegetable dishes or splashed on salads. The very strong vinegars and the very bitter ones, should be used sparingly, and only for external purposes.

Natural, organic vinegars are not the same as commercially processed and pasteurised products. In its most natural state vinegar contains living organisms. These naturally occurring creatures, as well as some enzymes and vitamins, are destroyed when vinegar is processed in a high heat process, such as pasteurisation. Descriptions of a couple of these little inhabitants of the vinegar barrel follow.

Vinegar eels: are frequently found in vinegar. This species of nematode worm is a natural part of many vinegars. These curious creatures can be seen near the surface of a vinegar which has been exposed to air. They resemble tiny thread worms, and are considered a harmless part of vinegar.

Vinegar flies: (of the genus Drosophila) lay eggs which hatch out into larvae that live comfortably in vinegar. They thrive on this acid brew, but are not a particularly appetising addition to vinegar!

Chapter Four

Vinegar's Historic Development

A s vinegar's virtues became known, its production spread throughout the world. Vinegar's use can be followed through the ages in many different times and cultures. It has been used for everyday cleaning and for specific medical ailments for at least 10,000 years. And sometimes, vinegar can be said to have actually changed the course of history. Some of the more intriguing vinegar uses, as well as some vinegar hints for today, follow.

THE ORIGINAL HOT ROCKS

W as vinegar the world's first bulldozer? Without vinegar, Hannibal's march over the Alps to Rome may not have been possible! The chronicles of the march describe the essential role vinegar played in the task of getting Hannibal's elephants over the perilous mountain trails.

Frequently, the tortuous passage across the Alps was too narrow for the huge elephants. Hannibal's solution was for his soldiers to cut branches from trees and stack them around the boulders which blocked their way. Then the branches were set alight.

When the rocks were hot, vinegar was poured onto them. This turned them soft and crumbly. The soldiers could then chip the rocks away, making a passage for both the troops and elephants.

You may not have an immediate need to relocate a boulder so your elephants can cross a mountain range, but you may went to try some of these ways to ease cleaning chores:

Renew old sponges by washing them in vinegar water, then soaking them overnight in 1 quart (1 litre) of water with ¼ cup vinegar added to it.

Use vinegar to clean away mineral build-up on metal. Just add ¼ cup to a quart (1 litre) of water for cleaning iron and aluminium doors, windows and furniture. Add extra vinegar if your tap water has a particularly high mineral content.

Clean windows with a chamois leather dipped in a bucket of warm water with two tablespoons of vinegar in it. The same treatment works well for windscreens.

- Spectacles will clean up more quickly without streaks or spots when wiped with water to which a splash of vinegar has been added.

Clean and freshen the microwave oven by boiling vinegar water in it. Mix ¼ cup vinegar and 1 cup water in a small bowl and heat for 5 minutes. This will remove lingering odours and soften baked-on food spatters.

- To remove badly burnt food from a pan, cover the burnt area with water and vinegar. Bring the pan to the boil, then leave to soak overnight.

To freshen up lunch boxes and other containers damp a piece of bread with vinegar and leave it in the box overnight.

Wipe down wooden cutting boards with full strength vinegar. It will clean them, cut through grease, and absorb smells.

Remove the smell of fish from plates by adding a tablespoon of vinegar to the washing up water.

A splash of vinegar added to rinse water will prevent water spots on glasses. It kills germs, too.

Make a brass and copper cleaner by combining equal parts of lemon juice and vinegar. Wipe it on with a paper towel, then polish with a soft, dry cloth.

When saving jam, peanut butter and mayonnaise jars to use again it can be hard to get rid of the smell of their original contents. Rinse them out in white vinegar and they'll smell good as new.

Use vinegar and rhubarb to revitalise iron pans which have developed rust spots. Fill the pot with rhubarb, add ¼ cup vinegar and enough water to cover the rhubarb. Boil for 1 hour and wipe the rust away

Clean pewter with a paste made of 1 tablespoon of salt, 1 tablespoon of flour, and enough vinegar to make the mixture just barely wet. Smear it on discoloured pewter and allow it to dry. Rub or brush the dried paste off, rinse in hot water, and buff dry.

Keep drains clean by pouring in ½ cup of baking soda, followed by ½ cup of vinegar. After about 10 minutes, run hot water down the drain. Keep drains odour-free by pouring ½ cup of vinegar down them once a week.

● Wipe all kitchen work-surfaces down with full strength white vinegar to clean them and to prevent mould.

Add a generous splash of vinegar to hot water and use it with a little soap, to disinfect baby's toys. Be sure to rinse well afterwards.

Add cup of vinegar to a bucket of water for cleaner floors. Or, after washing in the usual way, rinse floors with clean water to which a cup of vinegar has been added. There will be no soap scum to dull the finish.

A quarter of a cup vinegar added to a load of laundry, along with the usual soap, will brighten colours and make whites sparkle. This will also act as a fabric softener, and inhibit mould and fungus growth. It helps to kill athlete's foot germs on socks, too.

- Vinegar is a good addition to the washing machine when new clothes are being washed for the first time. It helps eliminate manufacturing chemicals and their odours.

A vinegar rinse will also stop static build up and reduce the amount of lint that settles on clothes. Some fabric stains can be soaked out in equal parts of milk and vinegar.

- A little vinegar and salt added to the water you wash leafy green vegetables in will float out bugs and kill germs.

When ¼ cup of linseed oil, ⅛ cup of vinegar, and ⅛ cup of whiskey are mixed together, they make a nice furniture polish. Dirt seems to disappear as the alcohol evaporates.

Wood scratches can be repaired with vinegar and iodine. Mix equal parts of each in a small dish and apply with an artist's paint brush. Add extra iodine for a deeper colour, more vinegar for a lighter colour.

A good saddle soap can be made from ⅛ cup of liquid soap, ⅛ cup of linseed oil, ¼ cup of beeswax, and ¼ cup of vinegar. Warm the beeswax slowly in the vinegar. Then add the soap and oil. Keep the mixture warm until it will all mix together smoothly. Then cool until it is solid. To use, rub it onto good leather, then buff to a high shine.

Polish leather with a mixture of ⅓ cup of linseed oil, ⅓ cup of vinegar, and ⅓ cup of water. Beat it all together and apply with a soft cloth. Then buff with a clean rag.

Vinegar can help to remove salt stains from leather shoes. Wipe the affected area with a mixture of equal parts of white vinegar and warm water. Polish the shoes immediately after application.

THE MOST EXPENSIVE MEAL EVER

The world's most expensive meal began with a glass of vinegar. When asked to think of the most costly drink, vinegar may not come immediately to mind. Yet it may take the prize for most expensive drink in history!

Cleopatra queen of Egypt, made culinary history when she made a bet that she could consume, at a single meal, the value of a million sisterces. To many, it seemed an impossible task. After all, how could anyone eat so much?

Cleopatra was able to consume a meal worth so very much by dropping a million sisterces worth of pearls into a glass of vinegar. Then she set it aside while banquet preparations were made. When the time came to fulfil her wager, she simply drank the dissolved pearls!

Cleopatra won her bet because she knew vinegar was a pretty good solvent. If you do not have an overwhelming urge to dissolve a few thousand pounds worth of pearls, you may want to apply vinegar's remarkable ability in some of the following ways:

Brushes hardened with old, dried-on paint may be softened by boiling them in vinegar. Simply cover them with boiling vinegar and let them stand for an hour. Then heat the vinegar and brushes until the vinegar comes to a gentle boil. Simmer for 20 minutes. Rinse well, working the softened paint out of the bristles. For an extremely heavy paint encrustation you may need to repeat the process.

Almost any old wood glue can be softened for removal. Simply wet the glued area with vinegar, and keep it wet overnight. Even some of the newer glues can be scraped away if they are soaked overnight in vinegar.

- Simmer ¼ cup of vinegar in a pot of water, uncovered, to clear the air of lingering cooking odours. Add ½ teaspoon of cinnamon to the water for an extra special air freshener.

Half a cup of vinegar in washing-up water cuts grease and lets you use less detergent.

Make a good metal cleaner by combining 2 tablespoons of cream of tartar and enough vinegar to make a paste. Rub it on and let it dry. Wash it off with plain warm water and dry with an old towel. The metal will gleam.

Clean taps and fittings with ⅓ cup of vinegar and ⅔ cup of water. Use it to polish and shine, or brush it into the shower head to remove calcium deposits.

- Combine ¼ cup of liquid soap, ½ cup of vinegar, and 2 gallons (8 litres) of water to make a great floor cleaning solution.

CAUTION: vinegar can dissolve existing wax on furniture and floors. Use very small amounts to clean and shine, stronger solutions to remove wax build-up and heavy dirt.

Remove ink stains from clothes by soaking them in milk for an hour. Then cover the stain with a paste of vinegar and cornflour. When the paste dries, wash the garment as usual.

Brass and copper will sparkle and any tarnishing will melt away if wiped with 2 tablespoons of ketchup and 1 tablespoon of vinegar. Polish until completely dry with a clean cloth.

Remove scale from an electric kettle by covering the element with a mixture of one part water and one part vinegar. Boil the kettle, then leave overnight. In the morning rinse with cold water, then boil one kettle full of clean water before using.

Clean and polish soft leather with a vitamin-enriched solution. Heat ½ cup of vinegar to boiling point. Drop in 3 vitamin E capsules and let stand, undisturbed, until the capsules dissolve. Add ½ cup of lemon or olive oil and blend well.

- Soak or simmer stuck-on food in 2 cups of water and ½ cup of vinegar. The food will soften and lift off in a few minutes.

Pewter cleans up easily if rubbed with cabbage leaves. Just wet the leaves in vinegar and dip them in salt before using them to buff the pewter. Be sure to rinse with cool water and dry thoroughly.

- Remove soap splashes from bathroom tiles with a mixture of one part white vinegar to four parts water — after applying rinse off and wipe dry.

Cider vinegar removes soap scum from more than just shower walls. Dilute it half and half with water and use it to rub down your body after a bath. It will leave your skin naturally soft, pH balanced, and free of soapy film. it also acts as a natural deodorant.

Remove light stains from marble with white vinegar. Wipe some on with a cloth, leave for two minutes, then wipe off again. Repeat the treatment if the stain persists.

● Nail polish will go on more smoothly and stay on longer if you clean your fingernails with white vinegar before applying the polish.

Perspiration stains in clothes will fade if soaked overnight in 3 gallons (12 litres) of water, to which ¼ cup of vinegar has been added. Use full strength vinegar to remove stains caused by berries, fruits, grass, coffee and tea.

● Another way to remove deodorant and anti-perspirant stains from clothes is to rub the affected area lightly with white vinegar before washing.

Dissolve chewing gum and remove stuck on transfers by saturating them with vinegar. If the vinegar is heated, it will work faster.

Clean hairbrushes by soaking them in 2 cups of hot, soapy water, with ½ cup of vinegar added to it.

Dentures will clean up easily if they are soaked overnight in white vinegar.

● Car chrome shines up fast if polished with vinegar!

Clean a dirty brick fireplace surround by scrubbing with undiluted malt vinegar.

When stripping walls of old wallpaper, let vinegar lend a hand. Make up a mixture of equal parts white vinegar and warm water. Apply this to the walls with a large brush or a roller. Leave for 15 minutes, then wet the walls again. The paper will come off easily.

- Keep a dish or two of vinegar sitting around when painting. The vinegar will absorb the paint smell. It will also clear the air and keep the room smelling fresh for a couple of days.

Use vinegar as a safe way of killing grass growing between paving stones — just pour undiluted white vinegar onto them.

- Azaleas love acid soil, keep them happy by watering them occasionally with a pint (600ml) of water which has a tablespoon of vinegar mixed into it.

To remove the smell of smoke from a room during and after a party put a small bowl of vinegar in one corner. It will absorb the smell of the smoke.

OTHER HISTORIC VINEGAR MOMENTS

The Babylonians, back in 5,000 BC, fermented the fruits of the date palm. Their vinegar, therefore, was called date vinegar and was credited with having superior healing properties.

You may know that vinegar is mentioned eight times in the Bible. (Four references are in the Old Testament, and four are in the New Testament.) But did you know there was a Vinegar Bible?

One famous version of the Bible is called the Vinegar Bible. In 1717 the Clarendon Press in Oxford printed and released a new edition of the scriptures. A mistake was soon discovered. In the top-of-the-page running headline of the 22nd chapter of the book of Luke, the word 'vineyard' had been misprinted.

Instead of 'vineyard' the printer typeset the word as 'vinegar'. The edition was quickly dubbed the 'Vinegar Bible'. And this is the name by which Clarendon's 1717 edition is known today.

Even poets have commented on vinegar. Lord Byron (1755-1824) called vinegar *'A sad, sour, sober beverage . . .'*

Well sour or not, vinegar's virtuous traits abound. Vinegar cleans by cutting grease. This makes it useful for melting away gummy build-up. It also inhibits mould growth, dissolves mineral accumulations, freshens the air, kills bacteria and slows its re-growth.

Many traditional recipes combine vinegar with other household supplies. Chemical company copies of traditional cleaners use synthetic chemicals that are not always as environmentally safe as more natural, organic compounds. Among the more popular substances which have traditionally been used in combination with vinegar are baking soda, borax, chalk, pumice, oil, salt, washing soda, and wax. To vinegar, add:

> **Baking soda** to absorb smells, deodorise, and as a mild abrasive.
> **Borax** to disinfect, deodorise, and stop the growth of mould.
> **Chalk** for a mild, non-abrasive cleaner.
> **Oil** to preserve and shine.
> **Pumice** to remove stains or polish surfaces.

Salt for a mild abrasive.

Washing soda to cut heavy grease.

Wax to protect and shine.

PLEASE NOTE: Some ingredients, when added to a vinegar solution, will produce a frothy foam. This is a natural chemical reaction, and is not dangerous in an open container. **DO NOT SEAL A FOAMING VINEGAR MIXTURE IN A TIGHTLY CAPPED CONTAINER!**

A collection of useful formulas for cleaning and polishing with vinegar follow:

Make your own kind-to-the-environment air freshener. Put the following into a plant mister: 1 teaspoon of baking soda, 1 tablespoon of vinegar, and 2 cups of water. After the foaming stops, put on the lid and shake well. Spray this mixture into the air for instant freshness.

Vinegar is an excellent window cleaner. Just mix ¼ cup of vinegar into 1 quart (1 litre) of water and put it in a plant mister. Spray it onto windows and wipe off immediately with clean, soft cloth.

An excellent furniture polish can be made from vinegar and lemon oil. Use 3 parts vinegar to 1 part oil for a lightweight polish. (Use 1 part vinegar to 3 parts oil for a heavy duty polish.) An oil and vinegar combination works well for cleaning and polishing. This is because vinegar dissolves and brings up dirt, and oil enriches the wood.

Dusting will go much faster if your dust cloth is dampened with a mixture made of half vinegar and half olive oil. Give furniture a new fragrance by cleaning with vinegar to which a little olive oil has been added. When the vinegar evaporates, the wood is left clean and beautiful — and smelling good!

Appliances sparkle if cleaned with a vinegar and borax cleaner. Mix 1 teaspoon of borax, ¼ cup of vinegar, and 2 cups of hot water and put it into a spray bottle. Spray it on greasy smears and wipe off with a cloth or sponge.

Clean brass and copper with 2 teaspoons of salt, 1 tablespoon of flour, and enough vinegar to make a paste. First, mix the salt and flour together. Next, add vinegar until a thick paste is formed. Then use the paste to scrub the metal, rinse, and buff dry. Add some extra salt for hard jobs, or some extra flour for a softer paste.

• Work surfaces will shine if wiped down with a mixture of 1 teaspoon of liquid soap, 3 tablespoons of vinegar, ½ teaspoon of oil, and ½ cup of water.

Once a week clean, disinfect, and deodorise wooden chopping boards. Rub them with baking soda. Then spray on full strength vinegar. Let sit for 5 minutes, then rinse in clear water. It will bubble and froth as these two natural chemicals react.

An excellent toilet cleaner can be made from 1 cup of borax and 1 cup of vinegar. Pour the vinegar all over the stained area of the toilet. Then sprinkle the borax over the vinegar. Allow it all to soak for 2 hours, then simply brush and flush!

Clean windows with ¼ cup of cornflour and ¼ cup of vinegar. Mix well and quickly dab it onto windows. Let it dry and rub off with a clean cloth. The glass will sparkle.

Make your own instant window cleaner! Combine ½ teaspoon of liquid soap, ¼ cup of vinegar, and 2 cups of water. Soak a sponge or small cloth in this mixture, then wring it out. Store the window cloth in a glass jar with a tight fitting lid until needed. Then simply wipe spots and smears from dirty windows. They will clean up without streaks — no mess, no fuss.

Shine and clean painted surfaces with 1 tablespoon of cornflour, ¼ cup of vinegar, and 2 cups of hot water. Wipe or spray it on, and wipe the paint dry immediately. Rub until it shines.

Preserve leather shoes and clean off dirt by rubbing them with a vinegar-based cleaner. Mix together 1 tablespoon of vinegar, 1 tablespoon of alcohol, 1 teaspoon of vegetable oil, and ½ teaspoon of liquid soap. Wipe clean, then brush until the shoes gleam.

Water scale build-up on glass shower doors can be removed with alum and vinegar. Mix 1 teaspoon of alum into ¼ cup of vinegar. Wipe it on the glass and scrub with a soft brush. Rinse with lots of water and buff until completely dry. (Alum is aluminium sulphate.)

- Soft vinyl surfaces are best cleaned with ½ cup of vinegar, 2 teaspoons of liquid soap, and ½ cup of water. Use a soft cloth to wipe this mixture onto vinyl furniture, then rinse with clean water and buff dry.

Remove light carpet stains with a paste made from salt and vinegar. Dissolve 2 tablespoons of salt in ½ cup of vinegar. Rub this into carpet stains and let it dry. Vacuum up the residue.

Remove heavy carpet stains with a paste made of salt, borax, and vinegar. Dissolve 2 tablespoons of salt and 2 tablespoons of borax in ½ cup of vinegar. Rub this into carpet stains and let it dry. Vacuum up the residue.

- Stainless steel cleans up nicely if scrubbed with baking soda which has been dampened with just a little vinegar.

Clean polish deposits off patterned brass surfaces using salt and vinegar. Make up a solution of one tablespoon of vinegar and one tablespoon of salt in half a pint (300ml) of hot distilled water. Apply the mixture to a small area at a time using very fine wire wool. Immediately after applying sponge the area with warm soapy water and dry it. If you leave the mixture on the brass; it will pit the surface.

• As with all cleaning products, test these traditional solutions to cleaning problems before using them. Always try them out on an inconspicuous area of rugs, upholstery, or clothing.

Cleaners you make yourself cost pennies, instead of the pounds supermarket cleaners cost. And, what is much more significant, the compounds you put together are safe, natural, and easy on the environment. Commercial equivalents cost more and may be more damaging to the environment.

Using vinegar to clean and disinfect is more than the inexpensive choice from a simpler time. It is the natural choice!

Chapter Five

Vinegar Making

For thousands of years cider vinegar has been made in much the same way. First, cider is made from a specially selected assortment of whole, fresh apples: they are washed, chopped, and pressed.

When the apple juice has been collected, it is allowed to age, sealed tightly away from the air. Natural sugars are fermented to produce alcohol. This cider is then allowed to ferment once again, while left open to the air. This time, the alcohol changes to acid.

- Originally the commercial production of vinegar was a by-product of the wine producer and the brewer. Vinegar brewing, as a separate industry, dates from about the 17th century. First established in France, it quickly spread to other countries.

Vinegar can be made from any liquid containing sugar, if there is enough sugar. Apple juice is one of the oldest liquids used to make vinegar, but grape and date palm use goes back thousands of years. Other popular vinegar sources are: black treacle, berries, melons, coconuts, honey, maple syrup, potatoes, grains, bananas, and even whey.

Wine vinegar has many of the same nutritional benefits as cider vinegar. After all, it begins with naturally ripe vitamin and mineral packed fruit. Wine vinegar will vary in colour, depending on whether it was made from red or white wine.

Vinegar's flavour, strength, and nutritional makeup depends on what it is made from. Sometimes 'Vinegar' is concocted from acetic acid (made from wood), coloured with caramel, and then called vinegar. This is incorrect (and illegal) labelling. Acetic acid does not have the food value or aroma of genuine vinegar

ALEGAR

One of the traditional vinegars made from a grain base is called alegar. Technically, it is a kind of malt vinegar. Malt is barley (or other grain) which is steeped in water until it germinates, then dried in a kiln for use in brewing. This malt is fermented into an ale. Ale contains less hops than beer, so it is both sweeter and lighter in colour.

The colour of alegar varies from pale gold to rich brown. The intensity of the colour depends on how the grain was roasted and dried. Medicated ales have been used for hundreds of years.

When wine or cider (from grapes or apples) is fermented, the result is called 'vine-gar'. When ale (from barley or other grain) is fermented, the result is called 'ale-gar'.

COMMERCIAL VINEGAR MAKING

Vinegar production usually starts in September and October when there are plenty of fresh ripe apples available. The first stage is to crush the apples to extract the juice. This may be done in either a hydraulic or a rotary press. If the press is hydraulic the apples will be pressed twice — a rotary press extracts all the juice in a single pressing. What remains of the apple is used either as a source of pectin for setting jams and marmalades, or to make compost.

The apple juice is put into large vats, usually made of wood. Normally Russian oak is used, as this is the best source of pieces of wood large enough to make these huge vats. Yeast is added and the juice is left to ferment, this takes about a month. The apple juice has now become cider. This cider is left to mature for about six months, then vinegar production can begin.

The process of acetous fermentation, or acetification, now starts. The traditional way of doing this uses huge 25,000 gallon vats. Into these vats is put up to two tons of sterilised birch twigs, These are steamed for two days, and then sprayed with a mixture of cider alcohol and freshly made cider vinegar from a previous batch. The vats are then left to allow the bacteria responsible for the second fermentation to grow on the twigs. Cider is then added and pumped through the vat for two or three weeks, until all the alcohol has turned to acetic acid.

The vinegar is then filtered and put into oak storage vats where it is left to settle, allowing sediment to be removed, and the flavour to mature.

For large scale producers, this traditional method has been superseded by two other methods which give equally good results. Indeed some people believe that these methods are superior since not so much of the volatile part of the vinegar is lost through evaporation. The methods are the Greenshields process, and Fring's Acetator.

In the Greenshields process the cider passes through a stream of air bubbles in a tubular feromenter. In Fring's Acetator the cider is filled with very fine air bubbles that remain in suspension allowing the bacteria to grow. The resulting vinegar is then diluted to reduce it's acid content from about 7% to about 5%. In a variation of the Fring's Acetator the vinegar produced is about 5% acid, and therefore doesn't have to be diluted. The advantage of this is that the cider vinegar contains a higher proportion of minerals and vitamins as a result.

However the vinegar is produced, it is usually necessary to treat it before bottling to make sure that moulds do not grow in the bottle, and it does not become oxidised. At one time the usual way to do this was to add sulphur dioxide, but even in small quantities this can cause asthma attacks in some people. Most manufactures now use another method, either pasteurisation, or the addition of acetic acid. The vinegar is then bottled, and is ready to be sold.

MAKE YOUR OWN VINEGAR

The are as many ways to make vinegar as there are apples, kinds of fruit, and people. If you have never made vinegar before you may want to begin with the first cider vinegar recipe below. Then, experiment with some of the other ways to make vinegar.

Vinegar making requires two separate, distinct fermentations. The first, called alcoholic (or vinous) changes natural sugars to alcohol. The second, called acid (or acetic) changes alcohol to acetic acid. It is important that the first fermentation is completely finished before the second is begun.

You can hurry the first fermentation along by adding a little yeast to the cider, and by keeping it warm. At around 80°F, 28°C the liquids will convert very fast.

To speed up the second fermentation, add a little mother-of-vinegar to the mix. And, the more air the mixture gets during this second part of the process, the faster it will convert to vinegar.

CAUTION: mother-of-vinegar (it starts the second fermentation) must not get into the liquid until practically all the sugar has been converted to alcohol.

- The vinegar bacterium is present wherever there is air. This is why any wine which is spilled at a vineyard must be mopped up at once. Bacteria could get started in the wine and sour it all! If a vineyard makes both wine and vinegar, separate rooms are used for each. And, barrels from vinegar making are never used for storing wine.

CIDER VINEGAR

B egin by making a good, tart cider. Combine sweet apples for aroma, tart ones for body, and a few crab apples for luck. The more sweet apples you use, the stronger the vinegar will be. This is because the higher sugar content of sweet apples produces more alcohol to change into acid. The more sour apples in the mix, the sharper the flavour will be.

Chop the apples and when they turn golden brown, crush them in a cider press. Collect the juice in a glass jug. Never use shop-bought apple juice to make vinegar. It contains preservatives, and may have been pasteurised, and so will not ferment properly!

Next, cap the cider jug with a small balloon. It will expand as carbon dioxide is released, while keeping air away from the mix. When the sugar is all changed to alcohol, it becomes cider. This takes 1 to 6 weeks, depending on the temperature and the sugar content of the apples used to make the cider.

It is not necessary to add yeast, as wild yeasts we always on apple skin and in the air. If a grey foam forms on the top of the cider, it is excess yeast, and is harmless. Just skim it off.

Finally, pour the cider into a wide earthenware jar, so there is a larger surface area than in a jug. Puts cloth over the top to let in air, while keeping out dust and bugs. Vinegar will be created in a few months.

Wild spores floating in the air will start the fermentation process, but adding mother-of-vinegar to the cider will hurry the conversion along. Simply smear a slice of toast with mother and lay it gently on the surface of the cider.

• Vinegar making works best if the ingredients are kept at around 80°F, 28°C. If the temperature gets very much higher, the bacteria needed for fermenting is killed. If the temperature gets much cooler than 80°F, 28°C the wild spores become dormant.

OTHER OLD CIDER VINEGAR RECIPES

Put cut-up apples in a earthenware jar and cover them with warm water. Tie a cheesecloth over the top and set in swarm place for 4-6 months. Then strain off the vinegar. For faster action, add a lump of raw bread dough to the jar.

Let this sweet cider stand open in a jug for 4-6 weeks and it will become vinegar.

Place apple and peach peelings, and a handful of grape skins, in a wide mouthed jar and cover with cold water. Leave in a warm place and add a couple of fresh apple cores every few days. When a scum forms on top, stop adding fresh fruit and let it thicken. When the vinegar is good and strong, strain it through a cheesecloth.

- Make vinegar in a hurry by adding brown sugar, black treacle, or yeast to cider.

OTHER VINEGARS

Let a bottle of wine stand, open to the air, in the summer sun. In about 2 weeks it will turn into a bottle of vinegar.

Make winter vinegar by letting wine stand open to the air for about a month.

Put 2 pounds (1kg) of raisins in a gallon (4 litres) of water and leave it in a warm place. In 2 months it will become white wine vinegar. Just strain the vinegar off and bottle it. Make some more vinegar by adding another ½ pound (225g) of raisins to the dregs and going through the process again.

Make a deeply coloured honey vinegar by pouring a gallon (4 litres) of boiling water over 5 pounds (2.5kg) of strained honey. Stir until all of the honey is melted. Then dissolve 1 cake (or package) of yeast in 1 tablespoon of warm water.

Spread the yeast on a dry corn cob (or a slice of toast) and float it on the top of the honey-water. Cover the container with a cloth and let it set for 16 days. Take out the corn cob, skim off the scum, and strain the liquid. Leave it to stand for a month or so, until it turns into vinegar.

Dark, strong-flavoured honeys will ferment much faster than light, mild ones. Add a cup or two of fruit juice or black treacle to the honey to speed up the change to vinegar.

Because the sugar content of honey varies a lot, you may want to check and see if your water to honey ratio is correct. Do this by dropping an egg into the mixture. It should float in the liquid, with only a small spot showing above the surface. if the egg sinks, add more honey. If the egg floats too high, add more water. This method should assure you that the specific gravity of the mix is about 1.05, the best for making good honey vinegar.

• For an extra special, clover-flavoured vinegar add a quart of freshly washed clover blossoms to the honey and water mix.

Dandelions add a unique taste to honey vinegar. Just add 3 cups of blossoms to the honey and water. Be sure to strain it before using!

Raspberry vinegar can be prepared by pouring 2 quarts (2 litres) of water over 1 quart (1 litre) of freshly washed red or black raspberries. Cover lightly and let stand overnight. Strain off the liquid and discard the berries. Now prepare one more quart of fresh raspberries and pour the same liquid over them. Let this set overnight. Do this for a total of 5 times. Then add one pound (450g) of sugar to the liquid and stir until it is dissolved. Set the mixture aside, uncovered, for a couple of months. Strain before using.

MOTHER OF VINEGAR

Mother (or mother-of-vinegar) is the term used to describe the mass of sticky scum which forms on top of cider (or other juice) when alcohol turns into vinegar. As the fermentation progresses, mother forms a gummy, stringy, floating lump. Mother is formed by the beneficial bacteria which creates vinegar.

Sometimes mother from a previous batch of vinegar is introduced into another liquid which is in the process of becoming vinegar. This use, as a starter for new vinegars, is why the gooey scum is called 'mother-of-vinegar'.

Sometimes as mother begins to form, it is disturbed and sinks to the bottom of the container. If it falls into the vinegar it will die, because its oxygen supply is cut off. This dead, slithery blob is called a zoogloea, and is worthless.

Mother sinks for two reasons. First, if the vinegar-making container is jolted, the film can get wet. This makes it too heavy to float. Second, if too many tiny vinegar eels develop in the liquid, their weight, as they cling to the edges of the developing mother, will weigh it down.

Over the ages, traditional vinegar makers developed a deep reverence for mother-of-vinegar. Often, some was saved from a batch of vinegar, then, it was transferred carefully to new batches of souring wine to work its magic.

Over time, this cultivated mother developed special flavouring abilities. It is still handed down, from generation to generation, and guarded as a secret ingredient in special vinegars. Tiny bits of the old mother are lifted out of one batch of vinegar and put into new batches.

● Mother-of-vinegar may also form on stored vinegar supplies. This slime is not particularly appealing, but its presence does not mean the vinegar is spoiled. Skim it off and use the vinegar.

While mother may not seem to many to be particularly appetising snack, some claim it is endowed with nearly miraculous healing properties. Some traditional mother-of-vinegar remedies follow:

Dip out a goodly spoonful of the mouldy mother-of-vinegar from the top of a vinegar barrel and eat it very slowly. This healthy slime will relieve joint pains and headaches caused by infections.

Rashes caused by infections may be made to go away by nibbling on the mother which floats on a good vinegar.

A bit of mother-of-vinegar, taken each day, prevents most infectious diseases.

Scoop the stringy mass of mother-of-vinegar from the bottom of a barrel that has held vinegar and save it for treating infectious diseases. Preserve it by mixing it half and half with honey. One small teaspoon of this honey and mother mixture, taken twice a day, gives protection from infectious diseases and parasite infestation.

Take a bite or two of mother-of-vinegar, morning and evening. It will keep germs and parasites away from the body.

Grow your own mother-of-vinegar, to hurry along home-made vinegar, or for nibbling, by combining one cup of vinegar and one cup of fresh cider. Put this, open to the air, to one side for a few days (or weeks, depending on the temperature). The scum which forms on the surface is mother-of-vinegar.

HOW STRONG IS YOUR HOME-MADE VINEGAR?

Commercial vinegar's acid content is standardised, but home-made vinegars can vary. What follows is one way to determine the percentage of acid in a batch of vinegar. You will need ½ cup of water and 2 teaspoons of baking soda, mixed together. Plus, ¼ cup of the water in which a head of red cabbage was cooked.

1   Put ½ cup of water into each of 2 clear glasses.

2   Add ⅛ cup of cabbage water to each glass.

3 Use a glass dropper to put 7 drops of commercial vinegar into one glass of the cabbage flavoured water.

4 Rinse the dropper.

5 Put 20 drops of the soda water into the same glass and stir well (stir with a plastic spoon, not metal). The water will turn blue.

6 Now mix 7 drops of your vinegar into the second glass of the cabbage flavoured water.

7 Rinse the dropper.

8 Add baking soda water to your vinegar (and cabbage water), 1 drop at a time. Stir after each drop. Count the drops.

9 When the colour of your vinegar water turns the same shade of blue as the commercial vinegar water, the acid content of the two glasses will match.

To find the percentage of acid in your vinegar, divide the number of drops of soda water you added to it by 4. For example, if you added 20 drops of soda water to your vinegar, divide by 4 and find that the acid content is 5%. (The same as most commercial vinegars.)

- The more soda water it takes to make your vinegar match the colour of the commercial vinegar you are using as a control, the stronger your vinegar is.

Chapter Six

In A Pickle And Proud Of It

Our world would be very different without vinegar's lively flavour to perk up humdrum foods. Each year, we use hundreds of thousands of gallons of vinegar. It is used alone, in pickling, and in innumerable bottled sauces.

The best vinegars begin with healthy, natural foods. Inexpensive vinegar, intended for industrial use, is sometimes fraudulently sold for preserving foods.

Cheap imitations are made from liquid sulphite waste from paper mills and acids from petrochemical sources such as oil, coal, and natural gas. Because grain and spirit vinegar is so much cheaper than food-grade vinegar (such as cider vinegar) there is a lot of financial incentive for businesses to use it.

In many countries there are also differences in the way taxes and import duties treat different grades of vinegar. Quality vinegar, from expensive food-base sources such as fruit juices, honey, maple syrup, apples, grapes, or even sugarcane or corn rates a higher tax.

• Different tax treatment goes back some time. The Revenue Acts established during the reign of Charles II charged different duties on beer and on vinegar-beer

Besides the differences in nutritional values, grain and spirit vinegars do not compare in taste to good, high quality vinegars. A high quality vinegar has a sour taste, without being bitter.

Pickling is one of the most basic, and easiest ways to preserve foods. It works by increasing food's acidity. Expect a batch of pickled vegetables to lasts month or two in the refrigerator. Or, over a year if they are tinned.

Because pickles are already partially preserved, they do not have to be tinned in a pressure cooker. A boiling water bath provides enough heat to seal and sterilise them. Care does need to be taken in choosing containers. The high acidity of the contents means that they tend to reacts with some metals, such as aluminium and iron. It is better to use enamel, glass, or stainless steel pans.

Even the water which is combined with the vinegar can affect the quality of the pickled food. Water high in iron or sulphur will darken foods. Be sure food to be preserved is of high quality, not bruised or damaged.

PERSONALISING TASTE

Everyone has their own idea of what the perfect pickle should taste like. There are several things you can do to adjust the taste: vary the kind of vinegar used, increase or reduce the amount of sugar, or change the spices.

There are some things you do not want to do in your quest for preserving the perfect pickle. Do not combat vinegar's tartness by diluting the vinegar excessively. This will lower the acid content of the mixture and could result in spoiled pickles.

It is better to mask tartness by adding extra sugar. Since sugar helps to preserve the food, doing this will not create a risk of spoilage. Use brown sugar and the entire batch will change to a darker colour. Use honey and the flavour will be heavy and rich.

Make simple cucumber pickles, or be creative and preserve aubergines, cauliflower, carrots, beans, onions, okra, Brussels sprouts, squash, or asparagus. Even fruits can be pickled.

Flavour your mix with oregano, bay, red pepper, turmeric, mustard seeds, dry mustard, garlic, basil, dill, peppercorns, hot peppers, onions, or garlic.

PICKLES

In some of these recipes cider vinegar is used, in others malt vinegar; others use a spiced vinegar, which may be sweet or not. The different vinegars give different tastes, but as far as their preserving action is concerned one is as good as another — only the acidity of the vinegar counts. So feel free to experiment!

- The exact amounts of spices, salt, sugar, and vinegar you use will depend on your own judgement. What tastes great to one person will be too sharp, or too sweet, or too garlicky to another.

The other important part of the preserving process is brining. Brining involves removing some of the water content of the food using salt. Brining is necessary because otherwise the water seeps out into the vinegar and dilutes it. This makes it less acidic, and therefore less good as a preservative. Brining can be a wet or dry process.

- Always use firm, young vegetables, because they make the crunchiest pickled food. And never store cucumbers for pickling in the refrigerator. They deteriorate if stored below 50°.

Wet brining works best with cabbages, cauliflowers and onions. Put them in a bowl and cover with a solution of 2oz (50g) of salt in a pint (600ml) of water. Allow one pint of this solution per pound (450g) of vegetables. Cover and leave overnight.

Dry brining works best with cucumbers, marrows and tomatoes. The sliced vegetables are layered and sprinkled with salt — about one tablespoon to a pound (450g). Cover them and leave them overnight.

Spiced vinegar

1 pint (600ml) cider vinegar
1 tablespoon of blade mace
½ tablespoon of cloves
½ tablespoon of whole allspice
1 x 3 inch (8cm) piece of cinnamon stick

Put all the ingredients in a saucepan, bring to the boil, then decant into a bowl. Cover with a lid and leave to cool for 2-3 hours. Strain the vinegar before using.

Sweet Spiced vinegar

1 pint (600ml) malt vinegar
6oz (175g) brown sugar
½ teaspoon of peppercorns
½ teaspoon of whole mixed spice
½ teaspoon of salt
¼ teaspoon of whole cloves

Put all the ingredients in a saucepan, bring to the boil, then decant into a bowl. Cover with a lid and leave to cool for 2-3 hours. Strain the vinegar before using.

- Never boil vinegar for pickles any longer than absolutely necessary. Acetic acid evaporates at boiling temperatures, leaving a vinegar which is too weak to do a good job of preserving.

Pickled Cucumber And Onions

Slice lots of cucumbers and small onions. Arrange them in a earthenware pot, in layers. Sprinkle salt over each layer. Add very cold water and put them on one side to become very crisp. While the cucumbers and onions soak, mix sugar, vinegar, and spices in an enamel pan. Bring the liquid to the boil and immediately remove from the heat. Drain the brine off the cucumbers and onions. Add the pickles to the hot spiced vinegar. Put the mixture into clean jars and boil. When cool, put the jars away for a few weeks before beginning to use the pickles.

- For the best taste, cut off the blossom ends (the opposite end from the stem) of cucumbers. There are concentrated enzymes in the flowering end of the cucumber that can soften pickles.

Pickled Onions

Put the onions in a wet brining solution (see above) for twelve hours. Onions tend to float, so put a plate on them to hold them down. Remove them and peel then put in fresh brining solution for a further twenty four hours. Remove from the brine, drain put into jars. Cover them in cold spiced vinegar (see above) and seal.

Red Cabbage

Take a firm red cabbage, cut it into four and remove the outer leaves and stalk. Shred it finely, and dry brine overnight (see above). Drain, rinse off the salt and dry. Put into jars and cover with cold spiced vinegar (see above) and seal.

Gherkins

Soak one pound (450g) of gherkins in brine for three days. Drain. dry and pack into jars. Cover with hot spiced vinegar (see above) seal and leave in a warm place for twenty four hours. Drain off the vinegar into a pan, bring it to the boil and pour over the gherkins again. Leave in a warm place for twenty four hours. Repeat the process two or three times until the gherkins are quite green. Top up the vinegar if necessary and seal.

- The salt used for pickling should always be 'pickling salt' or 'kosher salt'. They are both free of the iodine and starch often found in table salt. Iodine in the salt will darken the pickles, and the starchy anti-caking additives in table salt will cause the liquid to be cloudy.

Walnuts

Put green walnuts in a brining solution (see above) for a week. Drain and put in fresh solution for another week. Wash and dry and leave them exposed to air until they blacken (this should take a day or so). Pack into jars and cover with hot spiced vinegar (see above) either ordinary or sweet. Leave to cool, then seal. They are ready for eating in about 6 weeks.

Eggs

Boil some eggs for twenty minutes. Remove the shells while they are still quite hot and put them into a jar with cider vinegar, top up and seal. The vinegar prevents the eggs from becoming discoloured.

Piccalilli

6lbs (2.5kg) of vegetables — beans, cucumber,
cauliflower, marrow, small onions
1lb (450g) of salt
8 pints (4 litres) of water
8oz (225g) of sugar
1 tablespoon of dried mustard
1½ teaspoons of ground ginger
3 pints (1.8 litres) of cider vinegar
4 tablespoons of flour
2 tablespoons of turmeric

Slice the beans, dice the cucumber and the marrow, break the cauliflower into small florets, halve the onions. Make a brine solution from the salt and water. Put the vegetables in the brine, cover and leave for twenty four hours.

Remove the vegetables from the brine and drain. Put 2½ pints of the vinegar in a pan with the sugar, mustard and ginger, add the vegetables and bring to the boil. Simmer for twenty minutes. Blend the flour and turmeric with the rest of the vinegar. Stir into the vegetable mix, bring to the boil and cook for 2 minutes. Pot and cover.

● Remember, pickles pick up the flavour of whatever they are marinated in. This is what gives them much of their taste. Traditionally, pickled foods are served at the beginning of a meal because they stimulate the flow of saliva and gastric juices. This makes other foods taste better.

What Can Go Wrong With Pickled Foods?

Pickled foods are sturdy, able to withstand a lot of variation in the way they are processed. However, occasionally things do go wrong. The finished product is not perfect. Too strong or too weak a vinegar solution, or the wrong balance of sugar or salt can result in pickles that are not crisp and crunchy. Contact with minerals can cause pickles to turn unusual colours. Use the following information to identify the cause of pickling problems.

If	Pickles will be
Pickling solution (vinegar) is too strong	Tough
Brine is too weak	Soft
Table salt is used (it contains starch)	Cloudy
Pickling solution is too strong	Shrivelled
Too much sugar	Shrivelled
Too much salt	Tough
Cucumbers are old	Hollow
Cooked in a copper kettle	Off Colour
Insufficient time in brine solution	Slippery
Water has a high mineral content	Off colour
Cooked too long	Mushy

CHUTNEYS

Chutney making begins with British attempts to copy imported Indian preserves in the eighteenth and nineteenth centuries. People soon started to adapt the method for use with fruits that were readily available in Britain.

● When cooking a chutney you test whether it is ready by running a wooden spoon across the surface. If the mark it leaves takes a few seconds to fill with vinegar the chutney is ready.

Once potted, chutney should be left to mature in a cool dark place for at least three months. If you try a chutney that has not been matured like this you will find that it tastes too acidic.

Apple Chutney

2lbs (1kg) of apples
1lb (450g) of onions
2 pints (1 litre) of cider vinegar
1lb (450g) of raisins
1lb (450g) of demerara sugar
1oz (25g) of mustard powder
2 teaspoons of salt
1 teaspoon of cayenne pepper

Peel and core the apples, skin the onion and chop both coarsely. Put in a pan with the rest of the ingredients and bring to the boil. Simmer for about an hour, until the vinegar is absorbed. Pot and cover.

Green Tomato Chutney

1½ lbs (675g) of apples
1½ lbs (675g) of onions
4lbs (2kg) of green tomatoes
2½ pints (1.5 litres) of cider vinegar
2lbs (1kg) of demerara sugar
1lb (450g) of sultanas
4oz (100g) of sea salt
2oz (50g) of mustard powder
1oz (25g) of crushed garlic
1oz (25g) of ground ginger
1 teaspoon of cayenne pepper
The juice of 2 lemons

Peel and core the apples, skin the onions and chop both finely. Finely slice the tomatoes and put apples, onions and tomatoes into a pan with the rest of the ingredients. Mix well. Bring to the boil. Simmer for about an hour, until the vinegar is absorbed. Pot and cover

Dower House Chutney

1½ lbs (675g) of plums
2lbs (1kg) of red tomatoes
1½ (675g) pints of malt vinegar
2lbs (1kg) of apples
¾ lb (335g) of onions
4 cloves of garlic
½ lb (225g) dried fruit
1lb (450g) demerara sugar
4 teaspoons of salt
5 teaspoons of pickling spice in a muslin bag

Wash half and stone the plums, skin and slice the tomatoes. Put both in a pan with the vinegar and simmer gently until soft. Peel and core the apples, skin the onions, crush the garlic. Finely chop all three with the dried fruit, preferably in a food processor. Add to the plum and tomato mix with the rest of the ingredients. Simmer for about two hours, until the vinegar is absorbed. Remove the pickling spice. Pot and cover

SAUCES AND KETCHUPS

These sauces and ketchups need to be pasteurised to prevent them fermenting while they are stored. To do this you will need screw capped bottles.

First sterilise them by heating the bottles in a cool oven and soaking the caps in boiling water for 15 minutes. Fill the bottles with the sauce and put the caps on. Put a plate upside-down in the bottom of a deep pan and stand the bottles on it. Fill the pan with water until it comes up to the necks of the bottles. Heat the water to 170°F, 76°C, and simmer at this temperature for half an hour. Remove the bottles from the water and tighten the caps.

Green Tomato Sauce

2 small onions (skinned)
3lbs (1.5kg) green tomatoes
1lb (450g) of apples
½ pint (300ml) of cider vinegar
½lb (225g) of sugar
2 teaspoons of salt
1 teaspoon of pickling spice
½ teaspoon of dry mustard
½ teaspoon of pepper

Peel the onions and chop finely, along with the tomatoes and apples. Put with all the other ingredients in a saucepan and heat, stirring, for an hour. Sieve the mixture and discard the solids. Bring the sauce to the boil and pour into bottles. Sterilise and seal.

● Good sour, acidic vinegar causes saliva to flow. This increases our ability to taste and enjoy other foods. It also aids digestion.

Mushroom Ketchup

3lbs (1.5kg) mushrooms
3oz (75g) salt
1 pint (600ml) of cider vinegar
1 teaspoon of allspice (whole)
1 teaspoon of peppercorns
½ teaspoon of ground ginger
½ teaspoon of ground mace
¼ teaspoon of ground cloves

Wash and roughly chop the mushrooms. Put them in a bowl and sprinkle the salt over them. Leave overnight then rinse and drain. Mash the mushrooms and put in a pan with the other ingredients. Simmer, covered, until the vinegar is all absorbed (about half an hour). Sieve the mixture and discard the solids. Bottle, sterilise and seal.

- Sour tastes are one of the sensations the body is most easily able to detect. The sensitive sides of the tongue (the area where sour is registered) can detect one sour part in 130,000. But it is even more sensitive to bitter flavours. The tongue can detect one bitter part out of 2 billion. This sensitivity is a safety measure, to alert the body to poisons. It also makes cheap vinegars unpleasant to the tongue.

Plum sauce

4lbs (1.8kg) of plums
½ lb (225g) of onions
1 pint (600ml) of spiced vinegar (see page 81)
4oz (100g)of currants
½ lb (225g) of sugar
1oz (25g) of salt

Wash and stone the plums, skin and slice the onions. Put half the vinegar in a pan and add the plums onions and currants. Simmer for half an hour. Sieve and return the liquid to the pan. Add the rest of the vinegar, the sugar and the salt. Simmer until thick and creamy — about an hour. Bottle, sterilise and seal.

Chapter Seven

Cooking With Vinegar

A splash of protein, a dash of carbohydrate, and lots of vitamins and minerals — that's vinegar! A vinegary person is thought of as one who is ill-natured and sour. A vinegary food is apt to be one which has been changed from an ordinary taste to a gourmet taste. Vinegar's unique flavour perks up the taste of foods and keeps them safe from bacteria. Vinegar comes in dozens of kinds and flavours. Some ways to make and use flavoured vinegars follow, along with a few other interesting vinegar facts and recipes:

- Vinegar's acid softens muscle fibre in meat so it is tenderised. It also works on fish, salmon for example, and on lobster, oysters, fruits, and vegetables.

Vinegar helps break down tough cellulose, so use it on coarse, fibrous, or stringy cooked vegetables such as cabbage, spinach, lettuce, and celery. Sprinkle it on raw vegetables such as cucumbers, kale, lettuce, carrots, and broccoli.

Splash vinegar into bean soups, or use herb vinegar on pasta or bean salads to give a strong flavour without salt.

Because meat fibre is broken down and tenderised by vinegar, less expensive cuts can be used in most recipes. They are healthier, since these are the cuts with the least fat.

FLAVOURED VINEGARS

U nless directions indicate otherwise, all flavoured vinegars are made by adding flavouring agents to cider vinegar and allowing it to age.

Spicy Vinegar

1 pint (600ml) of vinegar
¼ cup of sugar
½ tablespoon of cinnamon
½ teaspoon of allspice
½ tablespoon of mustard
½ teaspoon of cloves
½ teaspoon of salt
2 tablespoons of grated horseradish
1 tablespoons of celery seed

Combine all the ingredients and bring to the boil. Pour over pickles or sliced, cooked beetroots.

Hot Pepper Vinegar

Add ½ ounce (15g) of cayenne pepper to 1 pint (600ml) of vinegar. Shake every other day for 2 weeks. Strain before using.

Celery Vinegar

½ teaspoon of salt
1 cups of chopped celery
1 pint (600ml) of vinegar

Boil for 3 minutes and seal it all in a glass jar for 3 weeks. Strain and use.

Chilli Vinegar

Add 1½ ounces (40g) of chopped chillies to a pint (600ml) of vinegar. Cap for 2 weeks and strain. For a super-hot vinegar, increase steeping time.

Cucumber Onion Vinegar

Slice 2 pickling cucumbers and 1 small onion very thinly. Add 1 pint (600ml) of boiling vinegar, 1 teaspoon of salt and a dash of white pepper. Seal in a glass jar for 5 weeks and then strain. Allow the sediment to settle and pour into a clean bottle and cap. The onion may be left out for a light vinegar that is especially good on fruit.

Horseradish Vinegar

Grate ⅛ cup of horseradish into a pint (600ml) of boiling vinegar. Seal for 3 days and then strain out the horseradish. Or, prepare an easy vinegar by simply putting a few large pieces of fresh horseradish in a bottle of vinegar. After 2 weeks, begin using the vinegar without removing the horseradish. It will increase in strength over time.

Onion Vinegar

Peel two small onions and drop them, whole, into 1 pint (600ml) of vinegar. Wait 3 weeks. Remove the onions and use the vinegar, very sparingly. A few drops will be enough to season most foods.

Nasturtium Vinegar

1 pint (600ml) of nasturtium flowers
1 pint (600ml) of vinegar
2 cloves of garlic (optional)

Combine and age for 6 weeks. Strain and use. May be improved by adding 2 peeled cloves of garlic.

Flower Power Vinegar

Add a flower scent to any vinegar by dropping in a few drops of scented oil. Or, add ¼ cup of strong herb tea to a pint (600ml) of vinegar.

Strawberry Vinegar

Crush 1 pint (600ml) of strawberries into 1 pint (600ml) of vinegar. Put to one side for 2 days, lightly covered; strain through doubled cheesecloth and discard the strawberries. Pour the same vinegar over another pint (600ml) of strawberries and mash them. After 2 more days. strain off the vinegar and add 1 pound (450g) of sugar. Boil for 10 minutes. A couple of tablespoons of this vinegar in a glass of water is cooling and refreshing.

Fines Herbes Vinegar

1 pint (600ml) cider vinegar
1 teaspoon of peppercorns
1 teaspoon of tarragon
1 teaspoon of basil
2 pinches of salt
2 pinches of sugar
2 pinches of thyme
1 pinch of pimento
1 pinch of dried horseradish
1 chopped shallot
1 crushed chopped bay leaf
1 leaf of rosemary
The grated rind of 2 lemons

Combine all the ingredients and mix well, Bottle and leave for two or three months before using in salad dressings.

Tarragon Vinegar

Put ¼ cup of tarragon leaves in a pint bottle of vinegar and leave for 8 weeks. Use on cooked and raw vegetables.

Garlic Lover's Vinegar

Separate and peel half the cloves of a large garlic bulb. Put them in a pint (600ml) of vinegar and allow to steep for 2 weeks. Strain off the vinegar and discard the garlic. Only a few drops are needed in most dishes.

Mint Vinegar

Stuff a bottle full of mint leaves. Then fill the bottle with hot vinegar, cap and put aside for 6 weeks. Strain and use with meats or in cool drinks.

Meat Flavouring Vinegar

½ large grated onion
2 red peppers, chopped fine
1 tablespoons of brown sugar
½ tablespoon of celery seed
½ tablespoon of dry mustard
½ teaspoon of turmeric
½ teaspoon of pepper
¼ teaspoon of salt

Stir all ingredients into a pint (600ml) of vinegar. Leave for 3 weeks. 2 tablespoons of this will flavour and colour a stew or gravy.

COOKING WITH VINEGAR

Vinegar Fish Broth

4 pints (2 litres) of cold water
1 cup of vinegar
1 tablespoon of salt
3 small cut up carrots
2 small sliced onions
4 thyme leaves

Bring the water to the boil in a large fish kettle. Add the rest of the ingredients and 5 pounds (2.5kg) of large pieces of salmon or trout. Simmer gently, until the fish is barely tender. Add a handful of peppercorns and a few sprigs of parsley.

● All kinds of fish are easier to scale if they are rubbed with vinegar and allowed to rest for 5 minutes before scaling.

Stuffed Peppers

Stuff large green peppers with coleslaw and stack in an earthenware dish. Cover with vinegar and leave for 4 weeks before using.

● When cooking poached eggs you can make sure they keep their shape by adding a few drops of vinegar to the water in the pan.

Vinegar Dressing

½ teaspoon of salt
½ teaspoon of paprika
⅛ teaspoon of pepper
½ cup of cider vinegar
½ cup of olive oil
1 tablespoon of minced pickles

1 tablespoon of grated green pepper
1 tablespoon of chopped parsley
1 tablespoon of dry mustard
1 tablespoon of sugar
1 tablespoon of tarragon vinegar

Mix well and chill. Serve with cold meats or heat it and pour over broccoli, artichokes, or asparagus. A vinegar sauce on vegetables and meats is a nice touch for hot summer days.

● When steaming vegetables add 2 teaspoons of cider vinegar to the water. The vinegar prevents the vegetables from becoming discoloured, and also reduces the amount of vitamin C which is lost in cooking.

Vinaigrette

Soak a split clove of garlic for at least 30 minutes in 1 cup of vinegar. Discard the garlic (or add it to soup). Mix in 1 tablespoon each of dry mustard and sugar; 1 teaspoon each of salt and paprika. Add 1½ cups of salad oil and mix well. Use flavoured vinegars to vary the taste.

Blue Cheese Dressing

Add one to four tablespoons of crumbled blue cheese to the vinaigrette for a blue cheese dressing.

Curried vinaigrette

Add a teaspoon of curry powder and some very finely chopped onion to the basic vinaigrette. Leave to stand for one hour before using.

● If vinaigrettes are made with high quality vinegar, you can use more vinegar and less oil.

Spiced Mushrooms

1 pound (450g) of fresh mushrooms.
½ cup of cider vinegar
1 teaspoon of soy sauce
1 teaspoon of hot pepper sauce
1 tablespoon of olive oil
1 tablespoon of ginger
3 cloves garlic, peeled and chopped

Blanch mushrooms in boiling water for 2 minutes, drain and pat dry. Put all ingredients into a jar with a tight lid and refrigerate overnight. Pile these mushrooms on spinach leaves and serve with hot garlic toast.

- When peeling and slicing potatoes some time in advance of cooking them, add a splash of cider vinegar to a bowl of water and put the potatoes cut potatoes in for a few minutes. When you dry them. they won't go brown.

Vinegar Salad

½ cup of salad dressing
½ cup of cider vinegar
1 tablespoon of sugar
1 cup of raisins
½ lb (225g) of bacon, cooked crisp and crumbled
1 cup of sunflower kernels
2 cups of chopped and blanched broccoli
Half a head of lettuce

Mix the salad dressing, sugar, and vinegar together and drizzle over torn lettuce, raisins, bacon, sunflower kernels and broccoli.

- Mustard you make up yourself from powder will taste better and last longer if you make it with cider vinegar instead of water.

Cherry-Pineapple Vinegar Cake

1 cup of milk
3 tablespoons of vinegar
1 teaspoon of soda
¾ lb (335g) of flour
¾ cup of butter
¾ cup of brown sugar
1 teaspoon of allspice
½ lb (225g) of crystallised cherries
½ lb (225g) of crystallised pineapple

Stir the vinegar into the milk, add the soda and stir briskly. Cream butter, sugar, and flour together and add the fruit and allspice. Fold in the milk and beat well. Bake in a well-greased pan at 350°F, 180°C, Gas mark 4, for 1 hour.

- If you're making a cake and find you are short of an egg you can use vinegar instead! Provided the cake is made with self-raising flour you can substitute one tablespoon of vinegar for one egg without affecting the cake. Don't replace more than one egg in a recipe though.

Chapter Eight

What's New?

Vinegar is a familiar ingredient in all sorts of sauces. In America 10% of all the vinegar made is used for tomato ketchup. Vinegar also adds its distinctive flavour to salad dressing, mayonnaise, and a variety of sauces. It is used to make pickles and to preserve foods ranging from eggs to fish. But of even more importance is vinegar's medicinal use. It is useful as an antibiotic, an antiseptic, and as a nutritional supplement.

Vinegar is not the only non-prescription health-improver making news in the 90's. All of alternative medicine is becoming more popular. Many people use some form of alternative medicine. Practitioners of alternative medical techniques are receiving more and more visits.

In most cases the cost of non-traditional medical care must be paid for by the consumer. The National Health Service and most insurance does not cover it. Of growing concern to health care professionals is the fact that 72% of those using alternative health care do not tell their doctors about it.

In America the government has responded to this new interest in old medicine by establishing an Office of Alternative Medicine. The new authority's first budget, of $2 million (£1.2m), is almost entirely dedicated to exploring the value of traditional remedies.

The American government's rush to validate traditional remedies is partly driven by a desire to cut rising costs. After all, traditional remedies are almost always low-tech, low-cost solutions to the common maladies of mankind.

Devotees of cider vinegar are not surprised to hear that improved nutrition is emerging as a major factor in controlling health care costs. It also is a large step forward in increasing the quality of life for many people.

Much new evidence suggests diet supplements may help much more than many doctors have been willing to believe in the past. This makes taking simple, naturally healthy cider vinegar look better and better! Some of the newest medical information about vinegar use follows:

DON'T SWIM WITHOUT IT!

Jellyfish stings are no trivial matter. They can easily land a swimmer in the hospital. The Medical Journal of Australia now recommends immediate dousing of fresh stings with vinegar, considering it '. . . *an essential part of the first aid treatment for . . . jellyfish stings . . .*'

In America The Massachusetts College of Pharmacy and Allied Health Sciences agrees with this approach, noting that without immediate treatment jellyfish and Portuguese man-of-war stings can cause nausea, headache, chills, or even cardiovascular collapse and death. Yet, they add, '*Venom can be inactivated with . . . vinegar.*'

Traditionally, vinegar has been the remedy of choice for treating all sorts of stings and bites. Stings of bees, wasps, jellyfish, and many other creatures can be eased by soaking the affected area in full-strength vinegar. For best results the vinegar should be applied immediately after you have been stung.

DOCTORS RECOMMEND IT FOR EARS

Our grandparents believed putting diluted vinegar in the ears would ward off infection. Now medical authorities have confirmed their wisdom. The American Academy of Otolaryngology (head and neck surgery) suggests using a mixture of vinegar and alcohol to prevent 'swimmer's ear'.

Infections, as well as itchy ears, are a common complaint in swimmers. Doctors specialising in treating these ailments now recommend using vinegar to prevent swimmers getting them. Simply dilute vinegar half and half with boiled water and use it to rinse out the ears after each swim. For a more drying solution, mix vinegar half and half with alcohol. This helps to prevent both bacterial and fungal growths.

The Journal of ET Nursing reports vinegar is so good for the skin it is being used to treat some post-urinary-surgery skin complications. When urine, which is often alkaline, leaks onto delicate skin surfaces, it can irritate or even burn sensitive skin. Vinegar's pH balance is very close to that of healthy skin. And so, vinegar compresses, applied to the skin, help restore its natural acid condition, neutralise leaking urine, and promote healing.

MICROBES & PARASITES DESTROYED BY VINEGAR

A recent university test on agents which can kill microbes said: '. . . *(vinegar) was found to be the most effective agent used, which completely inhibited the growth of the test organism . . .*'

Another report addresses vinegar's action on bacteria on vegetables intended for eating: '. . . *vinegar solution for 15 minutes exerted pronounced bactericidal effect against this organism.*'

- In Ethiopia, Addis University reports vinegar is being tested as an agent to kill food-borne parasites. Early results show vinegar does a faster job of destroying the parasites than any of the other test mediums!

VINEGAR FOR ARTHRITIS

The Journal of the American Dietetic Association, while remaining extremely conservative in recommending alternative medical solutions, has proposed the possibility that there is room for both approaches to health. An article on arthritis suggested nutrition professionals should be 'non-judgmental' in relating to patients using unconventional therapies (such as cider vinegar) for relief of the discomfort of arthritis.

Meanwhile, a national newspaper reports vinegar and fruit juice can beat arthritis pain. Vinegar is sometimes prescribed for those suffering from arthritis or rheumatism because it is rich in potassium. And potassium helps to relieve arthritic pain.

In America, according to the Wall Street Journal, vinegar is being combined with apple and grape juices to produce one of the hottest selling sports drinks on the market. This 'new' drink is reputed to ease arthritis pain, improve blood circulation, and tackle heart disease. 1 million bottles of this liquid, at $6 (£4) a bottle, are expected to be sold this year. Its secret ingredient? Cider vinegar!

IMPROVED CANCER DETECTION

A lso in America, Western Michigan University reports early test results which indicate vinegar can be used to increase the accuracy of conventional tests for cervical cancer. Adding the new vinegar-based test to the standard test allows medical personnel to '. . . *detect women at risk for cervical cancer who would not have been detected by the conventional test alone.*' The vinegar test is simple for technicians, low-cost, non-invasive, and safe for the patient.

CAN VINEGAR PREVENT ULCERS?

W ill new scientific research prove vinegar can prevent stomach ulcers caused by alcohol? Early studies, printed in the Japanese Journal of Pharmacology, indicate vinegar may cause the gastric system to secrete a natural stomach protective. This natural defensive action seems to protect the stomach from alcohol-induced damage. Most surprising of all, a vinegar solution as mild as a 1% concentration appears to offer 95.8% protection from these ulcers,

Much more research work needs to be done before the medical community is ready to recommend using vinegar this way. Results have been noted only in very controlled test situations, so far. Further testing needs to be done to determine exactly how vinegar works to build up the stomach's ability to protect itself from damage that can be done by excess alcohol. But there is a definite possibility this may be a future ulcer preventative.

VINEGAR CAN BE DANGEROUS!

Lead can be a serious health danger. Latest studies indicate vinegar can increase the possibility of foods being contaminated with lead. Many soft plastic bread wrappers have been found to have labels painted on with lead-based paints.

If vinegar, or foods drenched in it, are stored in these bags lead could very well leach out into the food. This can happen in as little as 10 minutes. The danger of vinegar leaching lead into food only occurs if the plastic bread wrappers are turned inside out, with the paint side next to the food.

• Some people report temporary stomach distress when vinegar is taken frequently. This is particularly a problem when vinegar (or vinegar-water) is taken on an empty stomach. Taking vinegar with honey may help to ease this problem.

Dental researchers have reported that excess use of vinegar (and other highly acidic liquids such as carbonated beverages and fruit juices) can cause loss of tooth enamel. The reports concentrate on damage done to the teeth of relatively young people, but caution should be exercised by anyone using vinegar on a regular basis. You may want to consider drinking your daily vinegar tonic through a straw, to limit its exposure to tooth enamel.

THEN AGAIN, MAYBE ITS NOT SO BAD!

The British Dental Journal published a study which showed that vinegary snack foods are among the least harmful to teeth! The study found that salt and vinegar flavour crisps (along with peanuts) were less bad for the teeth than high carbohydrate foods.

VINEGAR CAN BE FUN!

An American firm now produces some very special pickles. Called Upside-Down Cajun Brand Pickles, they come in rather ordinary looking glass jars. But, the labels are stuck on upside-down. This means, when the label is the right-side-up, the lid is at the bottom. Supposedly, keeping pickle jars up-side-down keeps the pickles fresher!

VINEGAR AND ANIMALS

Cider vinegar is a well known traditional remedy for many animal ailments. Recently farmers have shown increased interest in treating their animals using cider vinegar. Among the ailments it has been known to be helpful for are:

Cows —Arthritis and mastitis
Pigs — Farrowing fever and scouring
Goats — Acetonaemia
Horses — Lost appetite and equine influenza
Sheep — Twin lamb disease
It has also been known to improve milk yield in cows. Many racehorse trainers give their horses cider vinegar to keep them in peak condition — the horse *Noble Dancer* is a famous example of this. Following their example many other owners of highly-bred horses now give them cider vinegar regularly.

A NEW GENERATION OF VINEGAR

Until recently all vinegar was pretty much the same strength. Now Heinz in America has introduced a vinegar intended just for cleaning. It is twice as strong as conventional vinegar.

This is a white vinegar, not cider vinegar. It promises to make cleaning and disinfecting with vinegar easier.

- Note: The new Heinz vinegar is meant to be used for cleaning, not for cooking or as a diet supplement.

What Does Cider Vinegar Contain?

L isted below are the typical range of contents for 100ml of English commercial cider vinegar. The levels of each will vary within the range from one brand to another, and indeed from one bottle or batch to another, since they will depend upon the way in which the vinegar is made, and the fruits from which it is made.

Of course there are other constituents, but the quantities of these are too small to show up in this kind of analysis. French cider vinegars may differ quite markedly from these quantities. The reason for this is that they are made using a strongly alcoholic cider, which when converted to vinegar gives a very high level of acidity. The vinegar is then diluted so as to give about 5% acetic acid. The result is that the levels of other constituents are much lower.

Solid matter	1-3g
Acetic acid	4.5-5.5%
Sugars	0.4-0.5g
Mineral ash	0.2-0.35g
Tannins	0.002-0.42g

Protein	0.05g
Calcium	5-8mg
Copper	0.025ppm-0.01mg
Iron	0.05ppm-1.5mg
Phosphorus	4.5-6.5mg
Potassium	80-100mg
Sodium	3-12mg
Zinc	0-0.05mg
Ascorbic acid	0-150ppm
Nicotinic acid	trace-0.02mg
Vitamin B_2	trace

Appendix II

Useful Addresses

The names and addresses of the main English producers of cider vinegar are given below. Contact them for details of your nearest stockist.

Aspall Cyder House Products
The Cyder House
Aspall Hall
Stowmarket
Suffolk IP14 6PD
Telephone 01728 860 510

Martlet Natural Foods
The Coach House
The Maltings
Shepton Mallet
Somerset BA4 5QE
Telephone 01749 344 606

Appleford/Whiteways are both marketed by
A Kerry Ingredients
Clee Hill Road
Tenbury Wells
Worcester WR15 8HJ
Telephone 01584 810 366

Thank You!

Some of the information in this book carne from the generous help of others. Of particular help were studies and reports from the following:

Surgeon General's Report on Nutrition and Health; US Department of Health and Human Services; C. Everett Koop, MD, ScD, Surgeon General, US Public Health Service.

American Academy of Otolaryngology (Head and Neck Surgery).

American Journal of Hospital Pharmacy. College of Pharmacy, The University of Michigan, Ann Arbor.

Department of Cardiology, University of Helsinki, Finland.

Departments of Comparative Toxicology and Ecotoxicology; Food Hygiene, Instituto Superiors de Santita, Rome.

Department of Conservative Dentistry, Glasgow University Dental School.

Department of Food and Nutrition, Winthrop College, Rock Hill South Carolina.